Sara Wenger Shenk

11644092

THE FUTURE PRESENT

The Phenomenon of Christian Worship

By the Author:

INTRODUCTION TO THEOLOGY

THE FUTURE PRESENT

The Phenomenon
of Christian Worship

MARIANNE H. MICKS

THE SEABURY PRESS · NEW YORK

The Seabury Press
815 Second Avenue
New York, N.Y. 10017

ACKNOWLEDGMENTS

I wish to thank the following persons and institutions for making this study possible: the Trustees of Western College for Women, Oxford, Ohio, for a sabbatical leave in 1968–69; the Graduate Theological Union, Berkeley, California, for access to their associated libraries (and, in particular, the libraries of the Berkeley Baptist Divinity School and the Church Divinity School of the Pacific, where the staffs were exceptionally helpful); my friend Alice Lafuze, for typing the manuscript.

Fifth Printing

ISBN 0–8164–2109–9

Copyright © 1970 by Marianne H. Micks
Library of Congress Catalog Card Number: 75–103844
Design by Nancy Dale Muldoon

Printed in the United States of America

All rights reserved. No part of this book may be used or reproduced in any manner whatsoever without written permission from the Publisher, except in the case of brief quotations embodied in critical reviews and articles.

Christian worship sustains, as it were, an eternal, never to be consummated hunch: a heuristic vision which is accepted for the sake of its unresolvable tension. It is like an obsession with a problem known to be insoluble, which yet follows, against reason, unswervingly, the heuristic command: "Look at the unknown!"

—MICHAEL POLANYI

Space is the Whom our loves are needed by,
Time is our choice of How to love and Why.

—W. H. AUDEN

Contents

Introduction

Worship is an active verb. Like *love,* it refers to something human beings do. People who worship and people who love generally suppose that they know what they are doing. They assume that other people are doing something similar under the same name. But worship, like love, is a curiously difficult activity to talk about. If one asks worshipers, "What, precisely, is it that you are doing?" no one can say very clearly. One major purpose of this study is to try to discover what worship is.

Worship is also a general noun. Like language, it appears to be a universal phenomenon. But, as has often been observed, no one speaks language in general. He speaks Danish, English, Japanese, or Hindi. So with worship. It always makes itself known in a particular religious or cultural context. This study is therefore concerned with one species of the genus worship, namely Christian worship. Perhaps if we understand one form more thoroughly, we can then think more openly about other specific forms.

Current history provides four good reasons, I think, for yet another effort to understand the nature of Christian worship. Each of them not only gives Christians a new motive to reexamine what it is they are doing, but also offers the possibility of fresh insight.

The first and most obvious is the yeasty, ambiguous state

of our fast changing world. The meaning and significance of worship have been called into question by a complex set of cultural developments. On the one hand, participation in traditional public worship appears to be declining. More and more churches all over the country are half empty each Sunday morning. Nor is this only an American symptom. At its 1968 Uppsala meeting, the World Council of Churches acknowledged "a crisis of worship and behind it a widespread crisis of faith." Some people are concluding that worship has no future in a secular age.

On the other hand, some people are asking instead what kind of worship is appropriate to the new world we live in, what forms must evolve in response to the new era. Within the churches there is a rash of experimentation with new modes of worship. Beyond the churches, especially in the youth subculture, is an explosion of activities which many observers think are related to the worship they seem to supplant. The age of the emptying pew is also the age of the Happening, of the Trip, of the March.

It is easy to note superficial likenesses between, say, an antiwar demonstration and a religious rite. It is tempting to interpret these similarities glibly—as boding either well or ill for the future of Christian worship, depending on whatever fuzzy notion of worship one is operating with. The questions about the future of worship are legitimate and inescapable. They deserve discussion on the basis of some thorough agreement as to what we are talking about.

The second and third reasons for rethinking Christian worship are, I think, almost equally ambiguous. The Ecumenical Movement has given many Christians wider experience of patterns of worship and thus made possible a new breadth of perspective on the subject. But it also sharpens old problems of form and freedom, raises the old bugaboo of some coming Superchurch imposing banal uniformity on cherished variety and richness. Any imagined threat to one's own way of worship uncovers dramatically intense feelings. Honesty compels Christians today to ask themselves why. What have we at stake, if anything, over and above the security of the familiar?

Similarly the Liturgical Renaissance of the twentieth century has deepened understanding of the full Christian tradition. It has led to a new appreciation of a common heritage in worship, shared alike by Catholics and Protestants, by Anglicans and Orthodox, by Baptists and Presbyterians. Patient work by liturgical scholars has produced a tremendous body of new knowledge about the Christian past. These scholars have indeed achieved something approaching unanimity about the essential elements of worship in the earliest centuries of the Church. To some extent they have succeeded in drawing lay attention to these essentials. The phrase "liturgical renewal" no longer suggests just petty preoccupation with candles or vestments. It evokes instead concern with substantive issues—with the active participation of the people of God in the public work of worship, with the mutual interdependence of Word and Sacrament in the life of the worshiping community. But again, Christians when they are honest hear themselves asking, "So what?" Is our reason for doing something just an antiquarian one? What claim, if any, does the past make upon our present?

Fourthly and finally, the study of worship has the advantage of a new intellectual stance, of a style of thinking which may help us shelve our preconceptions and look with new eyes at that human activity as it presents itself to our gaze. To call this stance and style "phenomenological" demands further explanation.

Phenomenology is now well known as a form of modern philosophy which looks to the German thinker, Edmund Husserl, as a founding father. Originally confined largely to the European continent, the philosophical movement has spread across the Atlantic in recent years, settling especially in such university centers as Northwestern, Duquesne, and the New School for Social Research.

The "phenomenological method" has long aided serious thinkers in many academic disciplines, including the academic study of religion. The father of phenomenological study of religion was undoubtedly Rudolf Otto, a contemporary of Husserl. It was Otto's book *The Idea of the Holy,* originally published in 1917, which first called attention to worship as *the* distinctively religious phenomenon, something *sui generis* which cannot be reduced to propositions about prior beliefs or consequent ethics. Otto's own students and latter-day disciples include such historians of religion[1] as Gerardus van der Leeuw, Joachim Wach, and Mircea Eliade, all of whom have had an influence on this study.

The winds of any fresh thinking always blow beyond the preserves of the professionals, however. Gradually their currents are felt in the far corners of the culture. Just as existentialism became something of an intellectual fad a decade ago, so phenomenology (which is not unrelated) has threatened to do more recently. By using the vocabulary, a person who is not a phenomenologist either by training or party affiliation, may seem just to be jumping on the bandwagon, trying to give his work an up-to-date tone.

Recognizing this possibility, I have nevertheless risked calling this a phenomenological study because I agree with Maurice Merleau-Ponty, the foremost French phenomenologist. What is truly distinctive about the phenomenological method, he declares, lies as much in the attitude with which one approaches a problem as in thinking it through according to certain well-defined techniques.[2] Using the adjective in this broad sense, I have borrowed from phenomenology the following premises:

1. Sympathetic study of worship calls for suspending one's own beliefs and disbeliefs. In order to be free to discover what worship is, one must put a parenthesis around it, leaving on the outside (at least for the time being) questions of true or false, good or bad. This attitude does not pretend to an Olympian detachment, however, to an old-fashioned objectivity. As Nietzsche said: "Cold gray eyes do not know the value of things." [3] A phenomenological approach calls for the recognition that a phenomenon always appears to some-

one. That person's whole self—mind, feelings, and disciplined imagination—must participate in his efforts to understand it.

2. The major goal is to describe, as fully and systematically as possible, and in its own terms, that which appears in human experience as Christian worship. This means resisting any temptation to explain worship away, either by reducing it to something less than its full self (for example, by deciding in advance that only certain activities are "true" worship), or by adopting some external category of analysis (for example, the psychology or sociology or even theology of worship). What worshipers themselves intend to be doing, and what they themselves think it means are, on the other hand, part and parcel of what is being described.

3. Thought about worship has too long been paralyzed by tired old distinctions between its inner and outer, subjective and objective, individual and community aspects. The phenomenon of worship is here seen as including all of these. Whole persons (subjects, who are not divisible into bodies and souls) worship. As whole persons they relate—individually and collectively—to the object of worship.

4. With these presuppositions, I have felt free to draw on a wide range of historical evidence and of contemporary ideas to help illuminate one or another of the many dimensions of worship, and to offer a stimulus for further thought. I have also felt free to use loosely the terminology from various disciplines. Our English vocabulary is so limited in this area that to opt for precision is to opt for boredom. The terms "cult" and "liturgy" have both been used as equivalents for public worship, for example, and so (alas) has the vernacular redundancy "worship service" when it seemed best to convey the intended sense.

All worship appears to be essentially related to man's experiences of time and space. The classic claim of Christian worshipers that they are doing something appropriate "at all times and in all places" has therefore provided the basic structure of the book. In the first part we shall examine those elements of worship which seem directly related to a temporal axis—and therefore to be more dynamic. In the second half we shall look at those elements which seem more intimately bound up with the spatial character of human life—and therefore to be more static.

What we must describe in a straight line, however, we experience all at once. It seems to me that Christian worshipers experience at once a summoning of the future and a shaping of the present.

PART I

Summoning the Future

Chapter 1

AT ALL TIMES

ACUTE AWARENESS of time permeates Christian worship, and the measures of time its language. A rhythm of past, present, and future pulsates in familiar prayers and hymns: "Give us this day our daily bread . . ."; "The hour is coming and now is . . ."; "O God, our help in ages past, our hope for years to come . . ."; ". . . per omnia saecula saeculorum." What do these hours and days and years mean to worshipers in their own time?

According to the eminent historian of religion, Mircea Eliade, religious man has always found in his worship a way of coping with the terror of time. It provides him a means of escape from the tedium wherein all minutes look alike on the dial of the clock. It allows him to stop the clock in order to re-create "The Great Time" of the past. By reliving that sacred time, man can in effect start all over again.

Eliade develops this thesis, with minor variations and with copious illustrations, in many of his writings. Because of its importance to our question, the theory deserves careful attention at the outset. For we are surely a people preoccupied with time, yet unable to make peace with it. Our everyday idioms reveal our basic ambivalence toward this dimension of our living.

Most of us hear a bell ring at a certain time each morning, an alarm to say that it is time to get up. We promptly strap

1

little watches to our wrists to help us keep track of the time through the day. But there is never enough of it. We feel pushed by time, or we run hard to catch up with it. We demand time-and-a-half for overtime. Getting to school or to work on time is a cardinal virtue. Not keeping up with the times is a cardinal sin. So, in the recent past at least, was wasting time.

In the near future, so it is said, we will have more leisure time. How people will spend their time then is foreseen as a major social problem. Already some people have too much time on their hands, know it as a monotonous burden. In fact, they are just killing time. They have nothing to give significance to the relentless ticking of the clock.

Archaic and traditional societies provide Eliade with abundant support for his argument that worship has an answer to all this. The ancient civilizations of Asia and the Mediterranean have generously left their myths behind. The tribal societies studied by cultural anthropologists keep the mythic view of things alive today. Although Eliade sometimes uses the term "primitive" for such cultures, he does not share any of the condescension which is often poured into that word.

The myths of these societies are neither merely childlike stories about the gods, nor merely prescientific explanations of how the world and mankind came into being. They are rather the scenarios of religious drama, meant to be re-enacted in the present, allowing the community to participate in the reality that is given mythic expression. For, as Eliade never tires of saying, mythic behavior is "the expression of *a mode of being in the world.*" [1]

One ever-recurring myth, found in different forms but with the same essential structure, it is argued, concerns the Time of "the beginnings." It narrates the activities of supernatural beings who caused the cosmos. What happened in that primordial time (*in illo tempore,* to use a phrase Eliade is fond of) directly concerns man as he is today. That sacred history provides him with a model for the present, a paradigm for every kind of creative human "doings." Moreover, by re-enacting the old events "one again witnesses the creative deeds of the Supernaturals; one ceases to exist in the everyday world and enters a transfigured, auroral world impregnated with the Supernaturals' presence. What is involved is not a commemoration of mythical events but a reiteration of them. The protagonists of the myth are made present, one becomes their contemporary." [2]

The "religious experience" Eliade describes in these terms allows man, therefore, continually to regenerate time. By periodically re-entering the strong time of origins, by becoming contemporary with the creative act par excellence, he gives time a different quality. Most notably this regeneration is accomplished at the annual New Year's festival, an event widely documented by mythico-ritual scenarios from archaic and traditional societies. This occasion was understood as assuring both the fertility of the earth and the stability of the government for the full cycle of the coming year.

Since in mythological thought all life is a unity, however, the cosmogonic myth applied to all planes of life. Participation in the rite affected the individual as well as the community as a whole. It could reverse all sorts of negative conditions, physical and psychological, assuring rebirth and power to the worshiper. The childless woman, the depressed bureaucrat, the unlucky farmer, and the anxious student could all find re-creation through such worship.

Other recurring myths, including the myth common to many cultures of a god who is killed, appear to Eliade to deserve similar analysis as far as time is concerned. Even though these events took place long after creation, they are equally important to remember and to go back to. If one forgets what took place *in illo tempore* he is unable to find fulfillment in his experience of present time.

A view of time which allows man indefinitely to recover the past in this way, as Eliade well recognizes, is essentially antihistorical. It refuses to value new or unusual events which do not fit the archetypal model. If everything can begin all over again, man no longer has "to bear the burden of time." [3] He can wipe out the mistakes of history and start afresh.

Eliade is careful more than once to distinguish this mythological view of sacred history from that which developed in Judaism and Christianity, where time is conceived as irreversible: "Christianity, as the faithful heir of Judaism, accepts the linear Time of History. The World was created only once and will have only one end. . . ." [4] Or again, "For the Christian Jesus Christ is not a mythical personage: on the contrary, he is a historical personage. . . ." [5]

Although Eliade is thus too good a historian to put different religious phenomena all on the same plane, he remains convinced that all worship attempts to overcome time by going back. Christianity is not exempt. In an essay on "The Myths of the Modern World," originally published in 1953, he puts the matter forcibly: "Christianity, *by the very fact that it is a religion,* has had to preserve at least one mythic attitude —the attitude toward liturgical time; that is, the rejection of profane time and the recovery of the Great Time, *illud tempus* of 'the beginnings.' " [6] Ten years later he repeated virtually the same sentence in the final chapter of his book *Myth and Reality.* What Christians are doing in their worship, Eliade still contends, is participating ritually in the time which begins with the birth of Jesus at Bethlehem and ends "provisionally" with his ascension into heaven. They are thus breaking away from humdrum chronology "through a moment which opens out into the Great Time." [7]

In short, to use Eliade's own words, "liturgical Time is circular Time." [8] If this analysis be accepted, then the worship of Christians by its very nature is in conflict with the expressed faith of Christians that historical time has genuine significance. For on this reading, the time of worship is essentially a time of escape into the past.

It would be foolish to underestimate the weight of the past in today's Christian worship. In fact, much of the history of Christian worship strengthens the argument just summarized.

The earliest Christians naturally continued forms of worship inherited from Judaism. From the beginning they also added their own distinctive act, with a distinctive understanding of its meaning. Very early in the life of the community, these two elements fused into a single pattern of worship which has continued essentially unchanged to the present. Its outlines may have been obscured at certain times in history, and in certain parts of the community, but the continuity was never completely broken nor the original shape destroyed. Agreement about this basic pattern is the great achievement of contemporary liturgiologists.[9]

As we describe this pattern of worship which emerged and developed in the first centuries, the backward thrust will be apparent. The questions posed by Eliade and his school remain open ones, however. To what extent is the dominant focus of the act antihistorical? Or to what extent does it give both meaning and motion to man's ongoing experience of time?

How the earliest Christian community in Jerusalem worshiped is summarized succinctly in the Book of Acts. The sentence is quoted in almost every study of New Testament worship; but that is not sufficient reason to omit it here, because it so clearly expresses the marriage of the old and the new that gave birth to Christian worship. As the Jerusalem Bible translation puts it: "They went as a body to the Temple every day but met in their houses for the breaking of bread" (2:46). The translators of the New English Bible have managed to suggest that the disciples agreed among themselves to carry on with an already well-established routine: "With one mind they kept up their daily attendance at the temple. . . ."

Only Christians who lived in Jerusalem were able to do this every day, of course, since there was no temple available elsewhere. The author of Acts had a special fondness for that holy city and its temple, so he naturally emphasized what went on there. The other New Testament writers who say something about what the young churches did agree that Jewish forms of worship were not abandoned, but make it evident that the decisive forms were those of the synagogue rather than those of the temple.[10]

In Greece about the middle of the first century, for example, Christians assembled for prayers and hymns, for scripture reading and instruction. When the rumor reached the apostle Paul that they were behaving in a disorderly manner at these meetings, he promptly wrote to tell them how things should be done. That part of one of his letters to Corinth gives us some of the best, as well as some of the most puzzling, information which we have about the form of the primitive Christian service (I Cor. 14:23–40). The puzzling bit, Paul's references to the practice of ecstatic speech, will concern us when we come to the phenomenon of glossolalia. At the moment our interest is in Paul's clear statement about the purpose of these meetings. They have, he says, one purpose only: "to build up the Church" (14:26 NEB). The alternative reading of the RSV comes closer to a literal rendering of the Greek word he uses: they come together for "edification." In English as in Greek this word can carry the connotation both of education and of upbuilding (as in the cognate *edifice*). The Jerusalem Bible translator chose the expression, "for the common good."

Whichever translation you prefer, there seems to be no question but that Paul expected people to get something out of it, to use the vernacular which many modern Christians use in judging a worship service (often in the negative), and which many modern clergy try to tell them is the wrong criterion to apply. Furthermore, it is evident that Paul expected everyone present (except women, of course) to contribute actively toward that end, although not all at once. They were to take turns speaking.

The pattern of action to which Paul alludes in this part of his letter is akin to that of the Jewish synagogue service he had so often participated in. Although he does not here specify that there must be regular readings from scripture (Jewish scripture, of course, at this early date before the creation of the New Testament), he appears to presuppose this: "We read in the Law," he says (v. 21), quoting from it to bolster his point. It is the same Torah which he calls on for authority to keep women in the background. This word of God is neither the invention nor the exclusive property of the Corinthian Church, he reminds them.

In Asia Minor slightly later in the first century, according to clues from other Pauline letters, the content of Christian meetings for worship was similarly close to that of the synagogue. Christians are to teach and admonish each other. They are to sing psalms and hymns with thanksgiving to God. The word of Christ is to dwell in them (Col. 3:15–17). Since most of these Christians had learned to worship in the Jewish synagogue, it is not surprising that they continued familiar habits. But it is not always recognized that Christians have never abandoned their Jewish heritage in the twenty centuries since.

All essential elements of the synagogue service which Jesus himself customarily participated in at Nazareth (according to St. Luke's Gospel) were still practiced by third generation Christians at the end of the New Testament period (according to the Pastoral Epistles). Thus firmly embedded in Christian practice, they persist to this day in all parts of the Christian Church—the essential service of the Word of God.

The Lukan description (4:15 ff.) of Jesus going to his hometown synagogue on the sabbath day "as he usually did" gives us only part of that service; but it reminds us that this was a "lay" occasion, with responsibility divided among the adult males of the congregation. On that sabbath day as on any other, one of them undoubtedly read from the Torah, the sacred scroll of the Law. A second reading, a selection from the sacred scrolls of the Prophets, was assigned to Jesus.

As constant references to "the Law and the Prophets" throughout the Gospels indicate, only these two parts of the Jewish Scriptures existed at this point in history. The third section, the "Writings," had yet to be canonized. The synagogue custom of public reading from the two collections of sacred writings, one considered more ancient and in many ways more authoritative than the other, finds an obvious parallel in subsequent Christian practice of two regular scripture readings—one from the Gospels and one from the Epistles. Indeed Christians probably developed and organized their own canon of scriptures in conscious imitation of the Jewish precedent, seeing a parallel between Gospels and Torah, and between apostolic letters and prophetic writings; but this speculation lies beyond our present concern.

Following the solemn reading in the synagogue service there was a commentary on the passage applying it to the present. So Jesus interpreted the section he had just read from the prophet Isaiah. Since these first century "sermons" were customarily delivered sitting down, the actions of Jesus would not have been as remarkable as they sound to many modern readers, who picture him rather rudely interrupting the normal flow of sabbath worship. Rather one may properly think of him, without too serious anachronism, as the "visiting preacher" that day—at least up to the point where, in Luke's story, he stirs up more violent reaction to his sermon than most visiting preachers today achieve.

Constant ingredients in the synagogue service of the first century, then, were scripture reading and fresh interpretation of the reading—be it called Midrash, commentary, instruction, or sermon. The same ingredients are present in Christian worship at the end of the apostolic age when Timothy is admonished to "attend to the public reading of scripture, to preaching, to teaching" (I Tim. 4:13). They remain essential features of the characteristic act of Christian worship.

Prayer and praise, most especially the still-traditional eighteen benedictions or blessings of the name of God, and the chanting of psalms always framed the readings from the word of God in the synagogue. The psalms were collected originally for use in temple worship, but they formed the hymnbook of the synagogue as well, when that assembly became normative in postexilic Judaism. In the letter to the young bishop Timothy just cited, the author gives instructions on what kind of prayer shall be offered when men "lift their hands" (the characteristic Jewish posture for prayer). He concludes his fatherly advice with a prayer which includes phrases native both to psalms and to synagogue.

By this time the Church is acquiring relatively fixed forms of worship, along with relatively fixed statements of belief and relatively well-defined forms of institutional management. It is often noted as evidence of institutional hardening that the author of I Timothy is one of the few writers in the New Testament to use the noun translated as "religion" (I Tim. 3:16; 2 Tim. 3:5), which comes from the same stem as the verb "to worship." It is equally noteworthy that the author is denouncing those people who hold "the form of religion" but deny the power of it.

So far in describing the development of the central act of Christian worship, we have been acknowledging its debt to the past. Elements borrowed directly from the Jewish synagogue evolved into that part of the Christian practice now frequently called the Service of the Word. The earliest Christians, however, not only continued their old Jewish habits. They also did something new. The summary quoted from Acts called this "the breaking of the bread." To this day breaking of bread follows the Service of the Word as the second act in the full sacred drama which became the norm of Christian worship.

To call "the breaking of the bread" a new and distinctively Christian act demands instant qualification, lest it be misread as a gross oversimplification of the facts. What Christians did on this occasion was also influenced by Judaism, as countless historians have shown at length. This is not the place to reproduce evidence showing how this sacred meal is related to Jewish home worship, and to synagogue and temple worship as well. Nor is it the occasion to argue the question of whether Jesus's last supper with his friends was a Passover meal, a special religious fellowship meal, or just a sacred meal in the same sense that every meal eaten together by devout Jews was considered sacred.[11] Let us simply take for granted that "the breaking of the bread" is rooted in that last supper and there-fore in Judaism.

The act became new and distinctively Christian, neverthe-less, the first time it was performed after the first Easter. The intention was new. The meaning the worshipers found in the act was new. For from the earliest times of which we have any evidence whatsoever, the breaking of bread by Christians (even long before they were called that) was linked inex-tricably to the event of Jesus's death-and-resurrection. They performed the act in thankful response to what they believed God had *now* done in history. They believed that they met their Risen Lord in that breaking of bread.

Three examples from the abundant evidence in the New Testament will serve to underline this point. Since we appealed to three historical strata to support the case for continuity with Judaism, we will draw on the same variety of documents to show the newness of Christian worship also.

St. Paul's report in I Corinthians 11:23 ff. is of inestimable historical importance to Christians, being the oldest written account we have of what Jesus himself said and did "on the night when he was betrayed." Hence it is frequently noted that he introduces the report with the same words he uses a little later in his letter when he reminds his readers that he attached major importance to telling them that Christ died for their sins and was raised on the third day. These are words appropriate to the formal handing over of a received tradition.

However fixed they may already have become in oral tra-dition, however, the words in context also serve Paul's pur-pose of combatting Corinthian bad manners. His emphasis is on their "coming together" to do something together. If a man is too hungry to wait for late-comers before starting to eat, he should stay at home. If he wants to get drunk, he should drink at home.

The purpose of coming together, Paul says, is to "discern the Body" (11:11). As always, Paul pours multileveled mean-ing into that word. It is always the Body of the Lord, both in the sense of the broken body of the crucified Christ and in

the sense of the interdependent members of the new community of which he is the Head. The latter meaning is implicit
at this point in his letter, required by the context of his argument for unified action in eating together, and suggested by
carry-over from his assertion a little earlier in the letter (which
was read aloud to the people, of course) that they are one
body because they share the same loaf of bread (10:17). But
Paul's intention to stress the former shade of meaning is explicit: "For as often as you eat this bread and drink the cup,"
he tells them, "you proclaim the Lord's death until he comes."

The Corinthians were still celebrating the Lord's Supper
along with a full evening meal. The Mass or Eucharist was
not yet a separate occasion. Yet Paul's instructions about the
meaning of what they are doing fully support Josef Jungmann's claim that thought about the meaning of the Mass
must begin "with the mystery of our Lord's Passion and
death." [12] This death is central, then and now. For Paul and
for the Corinthians, however, it still packed the power of a
current event. He is talking about their announcing an event
not yet a full generation in the past. We might feel a like time
sense if we were told that what we are doing today is a loud
reminder of the Second World War.

In Christian understanding, the new event worth shouting
about through "the breaking of the bread" was always the
single death-resurrection event, however—never just the ex-
ecution of Jesus of Nazareth. The example of the Emmaus
story from Luke's gospel (24:13–35) illustrates this essential
Easter concomitant. Again it is necessary to remember that
Luke is writing after Paul, but drawing on oral tradition,
stories about Jesus which were told and retold by the Christians when they gathered together for worship, and which
took shape from retelling on such occasions. Luke alone chose
to put this particular anecdote into his narrative of what happened on that first day of the week after Jesus was crucified.

"That very day," he tells us, two of the disciples were talking about the things that had just happened, while they were
walking along the road. Jesus, the story goes on, came and

joined the discussion, but they did not recognize him. Not, that is, until he was invited to stay for supper. Whereupon "he took the bread, and blessed, and broke it, and gave it to them" (24:30). At that moment they knew who he was. So, in Luke's story, they rushed out and hiked seven miles back to the city to tell his other friends who were "gathered together" how he was known to them in "the breaking of the bread."

The gospel writer has given us the report of a "resurrection appearance," it is true. This is another of those bits of personal testimony cherished by the early community and recited as part of their good news that "the Lord has risen indeed" (24:34). But it is also a notable report of a Christian "worship experience." It is evidence that when Luke is writing his gospel—at least twenty years after Paul's first letter to Corinth was written and perhaps fifty years after the first Easter—the act of breaking bread together on the first day of the week was understood by the participants as an occasion for meeting and recognizing the same Risen Lord.

Luke's stylized repetition of the same four verbs—took, blessed, broke, gave—furthermore, supports the theory that we are here reading an account shaped by, and told for, Christians familiar with regular weekly thanksgiving for the Resurrection in a formalized act of The Breaking of the Bread.

Still within the New Testament, one encounters concern on the part of a Christian to explain exactly how the new cult is different from the cult of Judaism. The author of the treatise known as the Epistle to the Hebrews uses arguments which seem to us excessively tortured. His language is the language of temple worship in Israel. Accordingly he sets forth a theory of sacrifice. His metaphors are ambiguous enough to allow modern scholars to expound opposing ideas of his meaning.[13]

What is most significant for our present purpose is his conviction that the old worship forms have been rendered obsolete by Christ's death and resurrection. By establishing a new covenant, Christ established a new way of "drawing near" to God.

The phrase is a synonym for worship. The author is disturbed because some Christians are neglecting "to meet together" (10:25). "For worship" is implied. He exhorts them to lift their drooping hands (12:12). "In prayer" is implied. He urges them to offer to God "acceptable worship, with reverence and awe" (12:28). The model and channel for that worship is Jesus Christ, the Son through whom God has spoken "in these last days" (1:2). "Through him, then," the author says toward the end of his essay, "let us continually offer up a sacrifice of praise to God . . ." (13:15).

The new and the old combined, then, to produce the distinctive act of Christian worship. The early documents of the community show that Christians were aware both of continuity and discontinuity between what they did in worship and what their Jewish forefathers had done. They insisted that a new era had begun with the death and resurrection of Jesus whom they called the Christ. What happened to him was pivotal in their worship, and they thought of themselves both as meeting him in their breaking of the bread, and as offering their prayer and praise to God through him.

The historical evidence is insufficient to date with any accuracy the process by which the "breaking of the bread" was gradually detached from its context in the evening meal, and welded together into a single liturgy with the elements of the service inherited from the synagogue. Some historians speculate that the process was speeded by the demands of Christians who were household slaves and therefore had evening duties to perform. Others note the charges of drunkenness, sexual license, and even cannibalism leveled at Christian "love feasts" by critics of the new cult, and denied at length by second century defenders of the faith.

A famous letter to the Emperor Trajan, written about the year 115 from what is now Turkey, shows that Christians in that area were already gathering before dawn;[14] but evening Agapes continued, in the West at least, long after a separate Eucharist was instituted. Probably customs about times of worship developed at their own pace in different communities, just as different local customs developed about all other ways of worship. There was and remains more variety than uniformity in the details of Christian practice.

About the essential outline of what was to be done "in all times and in all places," however, there was substantial agreement in the Church, both East and West, from the beginning of the third century. The oldest evidence for the full liturgy comes from the document known as *The Apostolic Tradition* of Hippolytus, giving directions for corporate worship about the year 200.[15] Related if fragmentary ancient documents indicate a similar structure in the eastern half of the empire. Without too serious distortion of the complex picture painstakingly reconstructed by liturgical experts, one can say firmly that Christian worship achieved classical expression in the period of the early Church Fathers.

From the time of Constantine on to the Reformation—whether Christians met together in Rome or Constantinople, Athens or Jerusalem, Geneva or Wittenberg, the regular order of service on the Lord's Day was recognizably the same. It began with the Ministry of the Word, sometimes known as the Synaxis or the Mass of the Catechumens. It proceeded (after the dismissal of any who were not full-fledged Christians in good standing) with the Ministry of the Breaking of the Bread, sometimes known as the Lord's Supper or the Mass of the Faithful. Whatever the name for the total service then or later —Eucharist, Mass, Divine Liturgy, Holy Mysteries—this was the form in which Christians expressed their response to the God they believed drew near in that holy time.

The excursion we have just made into time past confirms Mircea Eliade's thesis that religious people return time and time again in their worship to the recitation of events which they believe affect their present. In Christian worship as in other forms of worship, great stress is placed on remembering what once happened, and on recapturing, even recapitulating, that event dramatically. This is most apparent in the consistent pattern of taking bread, blessing it, breaking it, giving it—in conscious imitation of what Jesus did on the night in which he was betrayed. It is equally apparent that what Christians are remembering is not just the Last Supper itself, but his subsequent death and resurrection. In this respect they go beyond remembering a bit of human history. The Easter focus adds a dimension which transcends time past. Christians at worship still hear Paul say that the death Christ died was once for all, but "the life he lives he lives to God" (Rom. 6:10). The tense is present.

At this point, I think, the myth of eternal return, even in the qualified sense in which Eliade applied it to Christianity, proves to be inadequate to a full understanding of what Christians do in their worship. He recognized, you recall, that as a historical religion Christianity nominally accepts a linear view of time; but he argued that in its liturgy it is caught up, willy nilly, in an antihistorical or circular view of time, continually regenerating the present with power from the past. He contended that worshipers escape from meaningless chronology by participating in the primordial time of creation, or in other but still ancient events in which the gods took part along with the ancestors.

Precisely because Christian worship did take its form in the days of the ancestors, precisely because it is still doing what was done *in illo tempore,* it opens onto a Great Time (to use Eliade's apt term) which is yet to come. Insofar as Christian worship remains rooted in its own history and faithful to its ancient liturgy, it not only recalls the past but also eagerly strains toward the future.

One of the sharpest distinctions among religions may well be what Ernst Cassirer has described as "the gestalt assumed by time as a whole." This pattern depends, he believes, "on how the religious consciousness distributes the light and shadow, on whether it dwells on and immerses itself in one phase of time or in another upon which it sets a mark of special value. Present, past, and future, it is true, are the basic factors in any picture of time, but the mode and the lighting of this picture vary according to the energy with which consciousness turns now to the one, now to the other factors." [16]

Cassirer examines some of the different gestalts to which the religious cultures of the world give expression. He finds that Hinduism, for example, seeks to annul time; sleep is the ideal in the Upanishads. In the Avesta, in contrast, sleep is seen as a demon; Persian religion, he believes, is oriented toward the future, just as prophetic Judaism was. Still another feeling for time is characteristic of Confucianism, which he thinks is so oriented toward the past that it aims only to perpetuate it.

If one follows Cassirer's attractive lead and looks for the gestalt of time expressed in early Christian worship, yet another picture emerges. One spotlight plays on the cross and another on the anticipated return of the Lord in power and majesty. Christian religious consciousness, partly no doubt under influences both from Persian and prophetic religious consciousness, oriented itself toward the End as well as toward its own beginnings.

Paul's letter to Corinth, already appealed to for so much evidence about the content of early worship, has again to be called on. For although he was writing in Greek, he included in the last paragraph an Aramaic phrase—*Marana tha,* "O Lord, come!" Commentators agree that it is unlikely that Paul would use a foreign phrase in writing to a Greek-speaking congregation unless he expected them to understand it. The general consensus is that the phrase must have been familiar from liturgical use, just as the other non-Greek words *Amen* and *Hosanna* were.

A very similar refrain appears at the close of the Book of Revelation. In that apocalyptic writing the Lord is repeatedly identified as Alpha and Omega, the first and the last, the beginning and the end. The Apocalypse (and thus the New Testament) concludes with the words: "Amen. Come, Lord Jesus! The grace of the Lord Jesus be with you all. Amen" (22:20–21). And in the early second century document called the *Didache* or Teaching of the Twelve Apostles, the Aramaic *Marana tha* occurs again, along with Amen. The context makes it almost certain that Syrian congregations were also using the phrase in their worship—"O Lord, come!" [17]

But it is already well known that these earliest Christians expected the imminent *Parousia* or "coming" of the Lord. Many of them expected it so soon, indeed, that they were especially grieved when any of their friends or relations died. Would he miss that Great Day altogether? Much has been written about the psychic consequences for the community when this vivid hope died. For some historians the phrase "the delay of the Parousia" became equivalent to "shattered illusions," and a catch-all slogan to account for the ills of a church condemned to carry on in history.

It is less well known that for centuries after their illusions are said to have been shattered, Christian worshipers kept their strong spotlight on the End. They appear today to be putting a new and even brighter bulb into it. The noted Dutch theologian E. Schillebeeckx, for example, declared not long ago, "Christianity is the religion of the Marantha: 'Come, Lord Jesus.' " [18]

As we have discovered in this chapter, Christian worship took shape in the past and continually reimmerses itself in that past—a time when worshipers were eagerly looking forward. In the next three chapters, as we examine in turn phenomena of motion, of calendars, and of speaking and hearing, we will also see how Christian worship still pulls toward the future.

Chapter 2

MOTION AND EMOTION

THE CALL for the renewal of worship in Christian churches today is a call to action. Critics of the comfortable pew deplore the fact that worship has become confused with spectator sports—indeed with something even less vigorous than watching a football game. Middle class congregations in the Western world, it is charged, are almost indistinguishable from the well-dressed, well-behaved (and passive) audiences at lectures and concerts. Christian worship in contrast, the liturgical enthusiasts say, demands that everyone get in the act.

Current Roman Catholic discussion of worship emphasizes full and active participation by all the people. *The Constitution on the Sacred Liturgy,* promulgated by Pope Paul VI in December, 1963, made it clear that the Second Vatican Council sought to promote such involvement.[1] Shortly thereafter, Romano Guardini, a father of the liturgical movement in Germany, noted that the fundamental issue in intense Council discussions behind that document was "the religious act underlying the liturgy," an act which requires not just "spiritual inwardness, but the whole man, body as well as spirit." He also wondered out loud if it is possible for modern man to rediscover "a whole world of acts which have become atrophied and are now to take on new life." [2]

Protestant writers share the same interest in recovering an

active sense of worship. One leading Swiss liturgiologist in the Reformed tradition, for example, insists that the celebration of the cult demands total engagement, because it is an action or "a game." [3] Such a word is startling to those who blame John Calvin for encouraging church-goers in Geneva to shrink the whole of worship up into the phrase, "going to the sermon." The English title recently given to a liturgical treatise by another Reformed scholar, *Dynamics of Worship*,[4] demonstrates that a vastly enlarged concept is at work when Calvinist theory speaks today.

To claim that Protestant worship suffers from "constipation of the bright emotions,"[5] moreover, is to forget the Christian third world. Many sectarian Christians today still witness to the interdependence of motion and emotion in worship, just as they have throughout the history of the church. People who use the derogatory term "Holy Rollers" for such sects seem to be unaware of the similar origin of the name "Quakers" for the now sober-seeming Friends, or of "Shakers" for that once disparaged group, now praised for its early American craftsmanship.

Most of us conveniently ignore contemporary gospel sing-ins, and dismiss the camp meeting as an outlet for emotionally starved frontiersmen. Our backward glance is so myopic that street corner frenzies in Massachusetts have no place in our stereotype of Jonathan Edwards, nor religious processions in our image of Geoffrey Chaucer. Movement is endemic in Christian worship, nevertheless; and such a perennial phenomenon demands serious attention.

If one seeks to describe the dynamics of worship, he finds it necessary to talk of ritual. The word poses a double problem, however. It automatically carries a negative connotation for many—particularly for young secularists who associate it with vain repetition, meaningless and deadly. At the same time, it can cause confusion even among those for whom it is a neutral term, because it has come to have a different meaning in the technical vocabulary of liturgical scholars from the meaning given it by historians of religion. For the former, a rite is the whole text of a liturgy, so that the associated actions are referred to as "ceremonies." For the latter, ritual is simply an agreed upon pattern of movement. We will be using it here in this broad sense, which Philip Wheelwright once summed up superbly by equating ritual with two or more children avoiding the cracks in the sidewalk.[6]

Ritual thus understood is a universal human phenomenon, not necessarily considered "religious" by those who practice it. Washing the family car every weekend or preparing a Thanksgiving dinner each November is a ritual in this sense. So are the stylized procedures of civil rights demonstrators, or of students marching about the administration building of a university.

In the following pages we will draw in turn on three different approaches to the meaning of such movement in general, in order to help us think more fruitfully about Christian ritual in particular. Ideas stemming from Maurice Merleau-Ponty, Friedrich Nietzsche, and Johan Huizinga all suggest answers to the question, "What is all this stress on action about?" Each man has already seeded fresh thought about active worship among those who are trying to understand it.

In Merleau-Ponty's thinking, the human body is fundamental to all experience. The human subject is always an incarnate subject. I don't just wear a body; I am embodied, and all my relations to the world are bodily relations. Merleau-Ponty continually reacts against both subjectivist and objectivist approaches to questions of body and soul. He denies, for example, St. Augustine's belief that truth inhabits the inner man, because "there is no inner man" which can thus be dissociated from the outer.[7] The mistake of intellectualism is seen as removing consciousness "from the stuff in which it is realized."[8] But by the same token, he rejects the empiricist theory which reduces all perception to external stimuli acting on the body. As the clinical evidence from countless amputee patients proves, I will still feel pain in my leg after my leg is cut off.

Closer to our present interest is Merleau-Ponty's further reflection that it is not simply my stationary body which perceives reality. I not only take a stand in the world, but I also turn my head to get a better view. By moving my body, I cause my surroundings to exist for me, much as the infant does by reaching for his toes and his toys. I do not continually turn around to make sure that the world is still behind me, but I certainly look forward to its being there tomorrow. Such metaphors of motion infest our language, supporting Merleau-Ponty's conviction that moving is essential to thinking.

His *Phenomenology of Perception* takes special note of two kinds of human actions which are sometimes felt to be a problem in Christian worship. It explores the meaning of individual gestures, and of established habits of bodily movement.

When I beckon to my friend, Merleau-Ponty contends, I am doing more than flexing a certain set of muscles. To think of my act simply in those terms makes the wave of my arm ridiculous. What I am doing with my muscles carries the weight of an "intentional arc." I am aiming at something. I am projecting myself. I am summoning my friend.[9] Similarly, my raised fist is not just "a weak translation of a prior angry thought"; it *is* my anger.[10] And when in due course a raised fist is thrust into my face, I do not decide upon reflection that it means that my opponent is angry. Instead I encounter an angry man.

What Merleau-Ponty means by an "intentional arc" in this connection is clarified by his discussion of so-called naive consciousness "when the unity of man has not yet been broken," in his earlier work *The Structure of Behavior*. "Our intentions," he says there, "find their natural clothing or their embodiment in movements and are expressed in them. . . ."[11] This, he adds, is why children say that thinking occurs in their throats.

Our bodies, then, speak a language of gesture. In every culture the language of gesture is an important mode of intersubjective communication. Philosophers have long been intrigued with it, and so have anthropologists. More recently some academicians have elevated the study of such movements into a science they call "kinesics," a form of biosocial communication shared by hummingbirds, honeybees, and human beings.[12] Merleau-Ponty would protest. He drew a sharp line between animal and human behavior, insisting that only men reach the level of symbolic conduct.[13]

If I should make a habit out of beckoning to my friends, or out of waving my angry fist, I would not be turning myself from a spontaneous person into an automaton. Instead, according to Merleau-Ponty's description of frequently repeated movement, I would thereby be "grasping significance." On his reading, habit is a way of understanding, a way "to experience the harmony between what we aim at and what is given, between the intention and the performance—and the body is our anchorage in a world." [14]

I get used to my new car, he explains, by being physically transplanted into it; or, putting it the other way around, I "incorporate" it, so that it becomes an extension of my own body. A typist, he observes, has "knowledge in the hands," and an organist in hands and feet. One could add that skiers, sailors, and other expert sportsmen also know intimately this kind of habitual harmony between their own movements and their intentions.

Such thinking about the kinaesthetic sense is relevant to the agreed upon movements which are Christian ritual, for here, too, a language of gesture is spoken. It cannot be translated into certain muscular contractions followed by concepts of what it means; nor, conversely, into some prior intellectual or spiritual insights subsequently expressed in motor symbols. The gestures themselves, as Merleau-Ponty says of speech, "accomplish thought." [15]

So the man who kneels down in the act of Christian worship does not think first, "Now I will be humble before the Almighty." He does not need an injunction to confess his sins "meekly kneeling upon his knees" in order to articulate the meaning of flexing those joints. Superfluous also is the catechetical information that this posture (together with clasped hands and a bowed neck) was construed by feudal lords to render even the most accomplished swordsman effectively *hors de combat.*

In the same manner, the man who leaps to his feet acts out,

without needing the words, the same intentions expressed in the ancient liturgical formulae: "Lift up your hearts," and (in the Orthodox tradition), "Wisdom! Let us stand erect." The movement itself is simultaneously evocative and expressive, both a summoning and a projection, of the whole person's way of perceiving his world and of being in it.

Furthermore, whether it is the agreed habit of a group of worshipers to make the sign of the cross at a given point in a liturgy, or to keep their hands folded in their laps, or to fling them up and ejaculate "Hallelujah"—the habitual actions are means both of drawing affective vectors and of acquiring motor knowledge of the world around them, a world which in the worshipers' living set of meanings includes the presence of the one whom they are worshiping.

All such movements change a person's hold on his world,[16] even if he is not able to say in other language how or why this is the case. In short, to borrow a phrase not found in Merleau-Ponty's writings, ritual in worship appears to be a prime instance in which the medium is the message.

Some messages never get delivered, of course, whatever the medium. We should not leave even this brief summary of some of Merleau-Ponty's ideas on movement without hearing his echo of Romano Guardini's question raised at the beginning of this chapter. Men should not *seek* to "perform significant acts," as did the seminarians in Stendhal's novel *The Red and the Black,* the French phenomenologist declares; such self-conscious effort, like false art, gives human life only a borrowed significance.[17] Nor should men expect a meaningful act to live forever, if the intentions which once vitalized it are gone. Our bodies may mimic for a time intentions which they no longer have, but such movement resembles the feeble gestures of an old man in an oxygen tent. Both comments are reminiscent of Paul Tillich's view that men cannot manufacture the symbols of faith, but they can allow them to fossilize. Such judgments flash a warning for those who want to revive old actions in worship and also for those who would like to invent new ones for a new age.

With Merleau-Ponty's help, we have so far been thinking about the individual bodily gestures which worshipers habitually make. Any given Christian service which presents itself for inspection, however, is a more or less unified whole, made up of many movements and gestures. It appears as an interwoven pattern of actions comparable to a drama. Partly for this reason, students of worship have long found additional help for their thinking in a classical distinction given classic expression just a century ago by Friedrich Nietzsche, whom Thomas Altizer has called the greatest prophet of the modern world.[18]

Nietzsche's youthful essay, *The Birth of Tragedy,* draws an extended contrast between qualities associated with the Greek god Apollo and those conspicuous in the cult of Dionysus. To Apollo belong the light of the sun at noonday, the bright images. He is on the side of law and order. "Apollo, as ethical deity, exacts measure of his disciples." [19] He demands self-knowledge. The calm of the sculptor, the restraint of the dance, the rationality of the dialogue are under his protection. Apollo "wants to grant repose." [20]

Dionysus interests Nietzsche much more. He is the intoxicated god, the mad one. He bursts out of nature with wild music, flies into the air in his dance. He brings ecstasy and self-oblivion. In his festivals, all norms were suspended; all the strains "of nature's *excess* in pleasure, grief, and knowledge became audible." [21] His votaries found themselves transformed through the excitement, able to enter into another body, another character—able to see the god.

Nietzsche was not the first to notice this contrast, of course. He borrowed not only the terms from the Greeks, but many of the insights they offer for aesthetic theory as well. His wholesale application of the two "hostile principles" to all forms of Greek art, and to culture in general, outraged a fellow philologist who found it unscholarly.[22] Later historians of drama, music, and religion have quarreled with many of his suggestions. One could well explore the close interconnections among dance, music, drama, and worship—and the persistence of Apollonian and Dionysian themes—without introducing this

controversial work which the author himself later found em-
barrassing.

I have chosen to appeal directly to Nietzsche, however, because he was not just describing another pair of "hateful con-
traries," as many second-hand allusions to his book imply. He
was proposing a thesis. The central argument of his essay
raises by analogy an urgent question for those who are thinking
about movement in worship. Nietzsche believes that tragedy is
born from the marriage of Apollonian and Dionysian elements
—and that tragedy dies when that union is dissolved. The duality itself, he writes, is "the origin and essence of Greek tragedy,
as the expression of two interwoven artistic impulses, *the Apollinian and the Dionysian.*" [23] When later dramatists tried to do
without the irrational, tried to make everything understandable,
he suggests, the poetry, the art, the drama degenerated. And
the rationality, too: "Because you had abandoned Dionysus,
Apollo abandoned you." [24]

By one of the ironies of history, Nietzsche addressed that last
remark to Euripides, his example of a dramatist who helped
to kill tragedy; Euripides wrote "The Bacchae," one of our
chief sources of information about Dionysian worship; and
in due course a modern Christian scholar used "The Bacchae"
to help prove that Dionysus has been barred from Christian
worship from the beginning. "All the very things which are
decisive for the Dionysian intoxication," he concludes, "are
radically rejected in the New Testament." [25] Such an overstate-
ment dwells on Paul's advice to the quarrelsome Corinthians
and plays down evidence of ecstasy in other New Testament
writings.[26] There has always been a Dionysian element in
Christian worship in Nietzsche's sense, even if some expressions of it have been systematically suppressed.

The neo-Thomist M. C. D'Arcy finds both elements present
in the Roman Catholic mass. His description of "the mystery
of love which the Christian sacrifice figures forth" makes the
terms Apollonian and Dionysian almost interchangeable with
agape and eros. Sacrifice seems to him always to be an expression of man's two loves.

With this understanding of a common element in all sacrifice, Father D'Arcy is not reluctant to embrace the symbolism of pagan religion, because he finds in it a dramatization of Christian experience. Moreover he sees that the Dionysian element in particular is ambiguous. This irrational "dancing out of doors to another's piping" [27] may be either above reason or below it. "This wild love" which comes sweeping into the temple behind Dionysus[28] may also be the love which draws man "out of himself to lose himself in the beloved." [29]

If it is not altogether clear when D'Arcy is giving Agape a Dionysian and when an Apollonian role, it is clear from his uses of the Greek imagery that he interprets the Mass with emphasis on the dramatic action of a sacrifice as a whole. Whether and in what sense Christian worship can be called a sacrifice at all is still an issue in Protestant-Roman Catholic dialogue, one seen to have major theological consequences. Although Father D'Arcy's discussion does not carry us beyond the old terminology of "inner feelings" seeking to complete themselves in the outward act, it does properly direct attention away from the sacrificial victim to the unified dramatic act in which it had a role. Furthermore he captures beautifully, as he describes the going in and the coming out which occur in the worshiper's experience, the kinaesthetic energy appropriate to Dionysian movement.

The Dutch Protestant Gerardus van der Leeuw also summons Apollo and Dionysus to inform his superb study of the holy in art: *Sacred and Profane Beauty*. All descriptions of the two gods, Nietzsche's and van der Leeuw's included, make their characteristic forms of dancing one chief point of contrast. Apollo's stately measures are countered by Dionysus's wild leaps. Dancing has always been a part of worship, and Christian worship is no exception. For, as van der Leeuw puts it: "The dance is the natural expression of the man who is just as conscious of his body as he is of his soul. In the dance, the boundaries between body and soul are effaced. The body moves itself spiritually, the spirit bodily." [30]

Evidence of ritual dancing in the ancient church is preserved in the Ethiopian liturgy; references to it remain in the hymns of other Orthodox liturgies.[31] In the Middle Ages the dance still had a recognized place in funerals and festivals. It survived at least until very recently in some Spanish cathedrals. Some of the Christian churches in Africa are making a place for it once again, if only to combat seductive drumming and dancing in rival sects.[32]

But the cultic dance, and particularly the Dionysian dance, have continually fallen prey to the Gnostic tendencies ever present in Christian life. David might dance before the Ark, but there was always some Christian Michal to despise him for it. In 1628 the Puritan Peter Smart was voicing a hoary suspicion of pagan ceremonies when he denounced the liturgical revival which John Cosin was promoting in Durham Cathedral: "Our youthful Apollo repaireth the quire, and sets it out gaily with strange Babylonish ornaments; the hallowed priests dance about the altar, making pretty sport and fine pastime, with trippings and turnings and crossings and crouchings. . . . Are these ceremonies fit for the Holy Communion?" [33]

We often forget that any ritual is the daughter of the dance. If the Christian Church in most places has successfully banished the frenzied leaping of Dionysus from its worship, it has carefully preserved the ordered movement of Apollo. As van der Leeuw argues persuasively, all the processions of Christian worship are relics of cultic dance.[34] When the choir marches down the aisle of a church, when members of the congregation walk forward with offerings of money or bread and wine, when the preacher solemnly mounts the pulpit or the priest carries forth the Holy Book—all these customary rituals are more than a way of getting from place to place without confusion. They are Apollonian movements ministering to what van der Leeuw sees as "the need to trace the complicated multiplicity of life back to a fixed foundation." [35] They promote the Apollonian mood which fills the soul with quiet.

Modern Western Christians should not try to revive the dance itself as a religious expression, van der Leeuw thinks— until they learn again truly to experience all dance. "But why," he asks, "should not mankind speak again in its most ancient language of the great mystery of movement and countermovement: the one movement which proceeds from this world to God, and the other movement which proceeds from God to this world?" [36]

A second constant in the contrast between Apollo and Dionysus is the contrast in their modes of music. Although the dance is all but dead in Western worship, music is very much alive. And the Apollonian sounds of Mozart and Bach, of the organ and Gregorian chant, have never quelled the Dionysian chorus.

One passage in Nietzsche's century-old essay strikes today's reader with peculiar force. He equates the Dionysian musician with the folk singer; but in folk song itself he finds the fusion of the two divine sounds. What is folk song, he asks: "What else but the *perpetuum vestigium* of a union of the Apollinian and the Dionysian? Its enormous diffusion among all peoples, further re-enforced by ever-new births, is testimony to the power of this artistic dual impulse of nature, which leaves its vestiges in the folk songs. . . . Indeed, it might also be historically demonstrable that every period rich in folk songs has been most violently stirred by Dionysian currents, which we must always consider the substratum and prerequisite of the folk song." [37] This university professor still in his twenties addressed the preface of this his first book to Richard Wagner, and gave it the full title *The Birth of Tragedy out of the Spirit of Music.*

The spirit of music in the Christian Church seems always to have been hospitable to the folk song, even if it has not always and everywhere welcomed the folk singer. The Negro Spiritual offers a good case in point. There is considerable evidence that much Christian hymnody comes originally from the song of the people.[38] The troubador strummed his lute and sang, "My heart is all confusion, this did a maiden sweet . . ." before the tune was baptized and given the new words, "O sacred head, sore wounded. . . ." A beloved Christmas carol and a minstrel's bawdy song are both at home in the rhythm of Green-

sleeves. The new birth of folk song in our own period, and its
welcome into Christian worship in some places, needs no
elaboration.

But we are still concerned just with rhythms, not yet with
holy sounds. What of the other Dionysian currents which
Nietzsche would expect to accompany guitars and drums? It
is increasingly evident that our secular culture is newly interested in bodily movement as such. Educators are discovering
that children learn through motion as well as through their
other senses. One theorist recently called for "Dionysiac ritual"
in the classroom, as a means of catharsis, a socially acceptable
period for releasing irritation, a scheduled time for stepping
outside oneself.[39] The Y.M.C.A. at a great university now
offers a course called "Community Through Movement." The
program of a national convention for psychologists not long
ago included a session on "The Rite of Movement," billed to
start "with each individual's rhythm" and to develop into a
"spontaneous group ritual."

Spontaneity is hardly the word one would associate with such
self-conscious efforts to rediscover ritual. One is reminded of
Merleau-Ponty's strictures against trying to invent significant
acts—and of the immobilized middle-class worshiper confronted with the demand to get up and do something. Is modern man just mourning a lost harmony of life, some primitive
past when rhythm was thought to constrain the gods?

The third in the trilogy of modern thinkers who have profoundly influenced reflection about worship suggests otherwise.
The historian Johan Huizinga places ritual action squarely
within the realm of play. *Homo Ludens*,[40] his seminal study of
the play element in culture, has become an inescapable point of
departure in present day discussion of game theory, whether
the theorist wishes to agree or to disagree with its author.

Huizinga readily establishes the formal similarities between
the sacred action of worship and any game. People play games
within specified boundaries of time and space. There is always
a playground. Thus the golf course, the tennis court, the card
table, the stage, the sanctuary share the features of a defined

sphere of activity. There is always a playtime also. Whether it be by blowing a final whistle, or by lowering the curtain, or by catching the last hidden child, or by extinguishing the last candle, people know when the game is over. They move back into "ordinary" life.

People often dress in special clothes for play also, thus heightening the separation between "ordinary" life and the play period. I put on my tennis dress or my magic cape or my choir robe, and become somehow a different person.

No one can compel me to play; Huizinga stresses this voluntary characteristic, the dimension of freedom in play. Yet once I step into this playing field, I accept its special order, its rules. So I am also constrained by the rules of the game, captivated by the play. I move in the designated rhythms; I carry out the prescribed motions. I "serve" when it is my turn to serve; I "move" when it is my turn to move. I don't go out of the bounds established by the Olympic regulations, the stage directions, or the rubrics.

Why? When we look for an answer to the why of play, we come face to face with two conflicting but not mutually exclusive theories. One school of thought says we play just for the fun of it; the other that it serves some purpose.

The first opinion dominates Huizinga's study. He is convinced that play is disinterested, in the proper sense of that word. My primary motive in playing a game is not the money I may win, figuratively or literally. I play just because I enjoy playing. In support of this view, Huizinga quotes directly from Romano Guardini's delightful description, in his early book *The Spirit of the Liturgy,* of the playfulness of the liturgy.

Guardini there defined play as "life, pouring itself forth without an aim." [41] The labor of artists, the play of children, and the public work (or liturgy) of worshipers are all of the same order. They are ends in themselves. They are "purposeless but meaningful." An even sharper version of the last phrase occurs in the English translation of the same quotation in Huizinga's book. There it is rendered as "pointless but significant." [42] So, to participate in the liturgy, as Guardini described it, means "foregoing maturity with all its purposefulness and confining oneself to play." [43]

Huizinga rightly recognized this as an idea influenced by Plato. It delighted him because it therefore did not belittle holiness by calling it play, but rather raised play to the level of a God-given gift. Both writers were pleased to be able to cite the wisdom of Proverbs 8:30–31 for evidence of the sheer playfulness of creation.

From the middle of the eighteenth century to the middle of the twentieth, however, as Huizinga shows in his skillful survey of Western civilization *sub specie ludi,* the play-factor in human life was increasingly subdued. A deadly earnestness infected all aspects of our culture, so that modern man finds it very difficult indeed to contemplate either art for art's sake or wasting time for God's sake. A built-in guilt at just having a good time now crops out in such protests as the one J. D. Crichton makes, probably with Guardini's and Huizinga's type of thought in mind, that the Mass is not just a playing before God, but rather purposive. [44]

When one proceeds to the question, "What, then, is the purpose?" one hears a variety of answers differing according to the religious or academic orientation of the speaker. I am impressed by the fact that they differ even more markedly in the way they align the purpose of play with the past or the present or the future.

One group continues to insist that the past dominates in all play. Some representatives of this group follow a psychological, some a sociological, line of reasoning. One current Freudian interpretation of play, for example, finds it grounded in the free eroticism of infants. On this reading play begins for all animals with the sensuous satisfaction of manipulating their own bodies, a satisfaction which human beings are forced to sublimate as they grow up. Adult games continue therefore as repressed remnants of infantile play. [45]

Virtually the same idea occurs in social dress, when it is argued that religious ritual represents a longing for the infancy of the tribe. Adolf Jensen's *Myth and Cult Among Primitive*

Peoples,[46] for example, takes explicit exception to Huizinga precisely at the point of time orientation. The two scholars respected each other to the extent that Huizinga cited an earlier work of Jensen's with approval to bolster one of his points, and Jensen in turn drew extensively on *Homo Ludens* to show that all the essential criteria of play are also hallmarks of cultic activity. He insisted, however, that what differentiates sacred ritual play from child's play is the time focus. Worship gains its sacred character, Jensen argues in unison with Eliade, by being a reminiscence of an elemental event in primeval time. He finds remnants of backward-looking cultic play surviving in seesaws, maypoles, tops, kites, and stilts.

Another set of theories about the purpose of play relates ritual play to the present. One plays for some immediate or almost immediate satisfaction. The old utilitarian approach to ritual which claimed that the "savages" by dancing around a mountain must be trying to accomplish something eminently practical, is thoroughly discredited today. The perfect squelch for such rationalism has been offered by Suzanne Langer, who observed that not even a rat in a psychologist's maze would continue to experiment with such ineffectual methods.[47] Nevertheless the play theorists continue to see some point in playing games, and so do the liturgists who espouse play theory.

In elaboration all of them seem to offer some variation on Plato's theory about the holy purpose of games, to which Huizinga appealed at the end of *Homo Ludens*. The crucial passage from the *Laws* is so pregnant for Huizinga, and for those who follow his lead in thinking about worship, that it must be quoted once again: "The young of all animals cannot keep quiet, either in body or voice. They must leap and skip and over-flow with gamesomeness and sheer joy, and they must utter all sorts of cries. But whereas animals have no perception of order or disorder in their motions, the gods who have been appointed to men as our fellow-dancers have given to us a sense of pleasure in rhythm and harmony. And so they move us and lead our bands, knitting us together. . . ." [48]

Included here is a theory of social utility. Play binds a community together. It establishes order.

One of Huizinga's recent critics believes that he made a fundamental error in failing to distinguish between play and games.[49] "Play" in this understanding would refer to the joyful but pointless activity of the very young, be they rolling puppies or skipping kindergarteners. "Games," on the other hand, would be properly reserved for ordered adult activity. This is a cogent criticism. It underlines the very point Plato is making, but which Huizinga ignored. Such a distinction, it is worth noting, is merely a variation of the Apollonian-Dionysian theme. In play-and-games, as in drama, there is a duality of movement. Sheer frolic is the mode of Dionysus. Orderly games by the rule book are in the mode of Apollo.

Finally there are some who think that the primary purpose for entering the sports arena has to do with the future. Games, as Huizinga saw, create a time of profound seriousness, a time of tension. The participants in a game are, as he puts it, transported into another world for a time. They abandon themselves "body and soul" to the game. The felt tension is thus partly between the ordinary world and the play world. It is also a tension straining toward resolution, toward the outcome of the contest, toward the end of the game.[50]

This, it seems to me, is essentially the argument which J. J. von Allmen adopts when he seizes upon and develops Guardini's idea that the liturgy is "an eschatological game." [51] "Worship is *par excellence* the sphere in which the future puts forth its buds in the present . . . ," he writes.[52] Christians who are acting out the presence of the Kingdom are learning to be receptive to the future, much it appears as children playing house or pretending to be firemen or nurses are anticipating adult roles. In Huizinga's apt phrase, implicit in von Allmen's view of playful worship, the gap between make-believe and belief breaks down in play. So Christians in their eschatological games are summoning the future.

In different ways but with inter-related results, then, Merleau-Ponty, Friedrich Nietzsche, and Johan Huizinga have all contributed in the past century to new thinking about worship. Each has sharpened attention to what human beings do—actively, with their bodies—in their rituals. Christians have appropriated ideas from the French philosopher to understand the embodied purposiveness of their moving about. He has made it vividly apparent that "going through the motions" of worship is a way of getting a hold on the world one is choosing to live in.

From the German philosopher, Christian thinkers have learned to recognize the different types of movement in their sacred act, which has its own dramatic rhythms. The Christian tradition clearly has included both the movement toward seizing and ordering life, and the movement of ecstatic abandonment to its mysterious powers. Reduced to simplest terms, these are epitomized in a child stamping his feet and a child skipping. Some believe that this duality is essential to express the fullness of Christian worship.

Transposing this insight into the language of childhood one can say that both play and games have kinship with worship. By stimulating thought about the playful character of ritual, furthermore, the Dutch historian Huizinga has opened the possibility that Christians are playing a game essentially directed toward the future.

One final lesson, taught by Nietzsche and Huizinga together, remains to be underlined. All thinking makes use of models. Neither the model of the drama nor the model of the game alone is a fully adequate model for the act of Christian worship, but the two of them together provide an indispensable insight into the dynamics of Christian worship. The act of worship is a total patterned action, with its own structure, coherence, and rhythm. Each of the worshipers in his own movements contributes to a larger and more complex group movement—to an act shared, Christians say, by "angels and archangels and all the company of heaven."

Chapter 3

RHYTHM IN THE CALENDAR

TODAY'S TECHNOLOGY plunges man into time in an altogether new manner. Unlike archaic man, modern man knows the enormity of the past—a past no longer measured by the eyeblink of human history but by billions of years of evolution. Again unlike archaic man, he is caught up in such rapid change that it almost overwhelms him. He feels propelled into the future at a much faster rate than he finds comfortable. When he contemplates his new capacity to program the future, including the future of human evolution, he shudders and is sore afraid.[1]

How can we achieve genuine selfhood in the midst of time as we now experience it? The question lies at the heart of one of the major philosophical works of our century. Martin Heidegger's profound reflection on the meaning of temporality, as much as any other aspect of his thought in *Sein und Zeit,* has earned him a place among the "makers of contemporary theology." John Macquarrie has suggested that Heidegger's idea of Being-toward-death is close to an idea of "eschatological" existence.[2] Authentic existence becomes possible when one accepts the imminent end. A boundary line of the future gives urgency and responsibility to my "ownmost" possibility. It shapes and unifies the myriad possibilities of my present life.

Most of us do not reflect on the meaning of time, however.

We feel more in rapport with Heidegger's predecessor in the treasure house of time, Augustine of Hippo, who introduced his reflections on the subject with disarming candor: "If nobody asks me what time is, I know; if I want to explain it to anyone who asks me, I am at a loss." [3]

In our unreflective living of time, we appear to know old rhythms in new ways which we would be at an equal loss to explain. Separated from any real dependence on seedtime and harvest, many workers in an industrial society tune their lives to the recurring cycles of weekends and annual vacations— two bright times to count on in the progress toward age sixty-five and retirement. This rhythm is already so well entrenched in the American way of death that it withstands a steady barrage of social satire without missing a beat.

The pattern of time in Christian worship belongs in such a framework because it is one of man's ways of Being-toward-death, one of his responses to the boundary line of the future. If we are to understand the Christian ways of observing man's weekly, annual, and life cycles, they must be placed in the midst of our normal experiences of time, both reflective and unreflective.

Historically and existentially, the weekend is the pivot of the Christian calendar. Weekends seem to us so much a part of the natural order of things, that it is hard to accept reports that they were not part of life in ancient Greece and Rome. The earliest Christians in the Western world worked every day, just as their pagan neighbors did; but they set aside time in one day each week to gather together in order to read the scriptures, offer prayers, and share the Eucharist. A Roman official noted simply that they met "on an appointed day." [4] The worshipers themselves had been taught to count it the first day of the week. They also learned to account it the Eighth Day. On both counts, they were consciously distinguishing their day for worship from the Jewish Sabbath.

Until the fourth century, when the Christian Emperor Constantine proclaimed it a public holiday and even excused his soldiers from duty in order to worship, Sunday was still a regular work day. Not until the sixth century was there a general requirement that Christians abstain from all work on that day. None of the Church Fathers identifies Sunday with the day of rest enjoined by the Ten Commandments.[5]

Confusion of Sunday with the Saturday Sabbath was a medieval development, accentuated, as H. B. Porter has shown,[6] by a theological confusion of Easter with Good Friday. Further accentuated by the Reformers' return to the Old Testament to bolster their arguments against Rome, it emerged in seventeenth century England as full-blown Puritan Sabbatarianism.

Against stringent Puritan demands to keep holy the Sabbath Day, King James I had a more ancient view of Sunday. He directed that after the end of divine service the good people of his realm not be discouraged from their "lawful recreations and honest exercises." Only such illegal sports as bearbaiting and bowling were forbidden. "For when shall the common people have leave to exercise," he asks, "if not upon Sundays and holy days, seeing they must apply their labor and win their living in all working days?"[7] The rhetoric meets warm response from today's Sunday golfer—until he notes the pragmatic arguments attached. If people cannot exercise on Sunday, the King observes, they may not be physically fit for military service. Furthermore, they may gather in alehouses, where discontent is bred by idle talk.

It is little wonder that many of his clergy refused to read this edict aloud from the pulpit as directed. They had found a better rationale. The already established Anglican method of combatting Puritan argument from Scripture was to turn to the Church Fathers. Patristic testimony proved to them that Sunday was not the Sabbath, but rather a day which gave Christians theological cause to rejoice.

The first day of the week was celebrated in the early Church as the Day of the Resurrection. The New Testament provides only circumstantial evidence: Jesus rose on the first day; thereafter Christians met together on that day of the week. The second century Apostolic Fathers connected this information. Ignatius, for example, speaks of the Lord's Day as the day on which "also our life arose through him and his death." [8] Justin notes that all make their assembly in common on the Sun's Day because on this day "Jesus Christ rose from the dead." [9]

In their efforts to contrast the first day of the week with the Sabbath, the early writers inevitably remembered other biblical associations. On the first day God began the work of creation, and so brought light out of darkness. The day on which Jesus breathed on his disciples and said, "Receive the Holy Spirit," likewise fell on the first day, according to the Fourth Gospel. Thus the Fathers soon found Trinitarian significance in the first day: it was already hallowed by God the Creator, Redeemer, and Sanctifier.

Some of them found another way of reckoning also. The first day may also be thought of as the Eighth Day—one day beyond the seventh day sabbath rest into a new creation, one day beyond the old weekend into a new ending of the weeks. The early Christian document known as the Epistle of Barnabas counts in this manner. The author interprets Isaiah's criticism of the old sabbath observance as God's way of saying: "I will make the beginning of an eighth day—that is, the beginning of another world. Wherefore also we observe the eighth day as a time of rejoicing, for on it Jesus both arose from the dead and, when he had appeared, ascended into the heavens (15:8b–9).[10]

"Barnabas" is drawing on a common apocalyptic image of the Coming Age. This image continued to be a favorite with Christian writers for at least another two hundred years, because it had the double value of helping them to distinguish between Christianity and Judaism, on the one hand, and to describe positively their idea of the New Israel, on the other. The Fathers were convinced that the New Age had begun when God raised Jesus from the dead. In one sense, therefore, the sabbath rest was over. God had started a new work. But the great sabbath rest was yet to come. They knew themselves still to be living between the Ages.

Thus in his "Dialogue with Trypho the Jew," Justin uses the fact that the First Day is also called the Eighth to prove typologically that Christians have the true circumcision, since the old circumcision was scheduled for the eighth day after the birth of a child.[11] In fact, as Jungmann observes,[12] any mention of the number eight in Scripture could bring forth allegorical exegesis on the Eighth Day of the new creation.

In a homily still included in the Roman Breviary, for example, Bishop Ambrose of Milan decides that there are eight beatitudes because eight signifies "the completion and fulfillment of our hope."[13] The same numerology is also alive in the East in the fourth century. In his treatise "On the Holy Spirit," Basil of Cappadocia takes off from the numbers one and eight in some Psalm titles to explain Sunday. Christians stand for Sunday prayer, he says, because the day seems to be "in some sense an image of the age which we expect."[14]

A few years later in North Africa Augustine takes a more critical view of the numbers game; but he is still willing to use numerical similitudes in answering questions about worship. His letter on the subject to one Janarius concludes: "The whole Church, therefore, while here in the conditions of pilgrimage and mortality, expects that to be accomplished in her at the end of the world which has been shown first in the body of our Lord Jesus Christ. . . ."[15] He returns to this theme in the final pages of his *City of God,* where he is describing life in the Kingdom when the pilgrimage is over. Then we shall ourselves be the seventh day, he says; for there we shall be still and know that he is God. That Sabbath will not be brought to a close by an evening but "by the Lord's Day, as an eighth and eternal day, consecrated by the resurrection of Christ."[16]

In "Barnabas" the Eighth Day was part of an apocalyptic vocabulary, with Sunday the foretaste of the imminent end. The idea of the Eighth Day popular with the Fathers in the fourth and fifth centuries still carried with it an essential eschatological reference. In our own day expositions of the meaning of Sunday have notably revived that two-way pull expressed by "Barnabas" when he said that the righteous man "both walks in this world and anticipates the holy aeon." [17]

Von Allmen, to cite one example, says that Sunday "restores time to its true end." He thinks that "Protestant moans on the theme of the desecration of Sunday . . . are stupid as long as the Church itself profanes Sunday by tearing out its heart: the celebration of the Eucharist." [18] But he also argues against celebrating the Eucharist on weekdays because such everydayness neutralizes the tension proper to Sunday, and suggests wrongly that the Church is already living wholly in the future aeon.

Reaffirming a day on which all Christians should hear the Word of God and take part in the Eucharist, the Roman Catholic *Constitution on the Sacred Liturgy*—to cite another example—recognized the eschatological character of Sunday by quoting the New Testament. Christians come together into one place on that special day of the weekend to thank God who has "begotten them again through the resurrection of Jesus Christ from the dead, unto a living hope." [19]

For Christian worshipers, then, Sunday remains radically different from the Sabbath. Whereas a contemporary Jewish scholar summarizes the meaning of the Sabbath for modern man in the magnificent and appealing phrase "an exodus from tension," [20] a Christian writer speaks instead of "the weekly disturbance occasioned by Sunday." [21] The day is seen as essentially a repeated entry into tension—an eschatological tension between the already and the not-yet. It is a day on which Christians rejoice and give thanks for the resurrection of Jesus Christ, for God's new creation, but also a day on which they acknowledge the urgency and responsibility which the End imposes.

Western urban culture provides rhythm not only on a week by week basis, we said earlier, but also on an annual basis revolving around the vacation period. Even the most cursory reflection about the calendar shows that the year as such now has very little "biocosmic" or social unity. A pluralistic society finds a common rhythm chiefly through shared celebration of holidays. Yet in very large measure individuals remain free to determine the decisive tempo of their own year.

To be sure, the time it takes the earth to make one revolution around the sun still has some influence on the experience of each twelve month cycle. Natural seasons continue to affect people, even people not directly involved with agriculture. My government fails to convince me that the New Year begins on January 1 with the civil year, and my employer fails to convince me that it begins on July 1 with his fiscal year, because I know in my bones that it begins with the first crocus in my garden. But even that vestigial sense of the year's rootedness in nature is hard to sustain when someone lives in a concrete jungle.

A man's work now seems to determine his "seasons" far more than nature does. It is apparent therefore that the members of our society do not all experience the same significant rhythms in a year. Whereas my calendar is governed by the "academic year" (restructured by committee almost annually), that of my C.P.A. neighbor is dominated by the "tax year" (changed by bureaucrats with equal frequency). Examples of seasonal variations among other jobs could easily be multiplied. Only a common round of legal holidays duly determined by civil authority creates some common national perception of the calendar, although the greeting card industry now greatly assists the government in this matter. Whatever one's geography or job, he watches drug store displays change rhythmically from Valentine red to Mother's Day pink, on to Great Pumpkin orange, and around again to St. Patrick's green.

Confronted by a plurality of man-made years, then, we are free to impose our own meanings on the year, to choose our own significant times. That special calendar known to Christian worshipers as the Church Year appears in secular society as one option among many for making ongoing time significant.

Like the other years which modern man experiences, the Church Year is linked to nature only in a very limited way.

Easter and Christmas, it is true, have often been characterized as baptized versions of nature festivals. Such celebration of the vernal equinox and winter solstice, it is alleged, is a ubiquitous human phenomenon. Although there is considerable basis for this idea, it does less than full justice both to the historical facts and to the interpretations Christians have given to them through the centuries. Since Easter has priority over Christmas both historically and theologically in Christian experience, we will consider this festival before turning to the logically prior feasts of the Incarnation.

As is well known, the annual celebration of the Feast of the Resurrection was closely connected with the Jewish feast of the Passover. The Passover was in turn closely connected with a prior Canaanite festival at the time of the winter barley harvest. Since an agrarian festival at the end of winter "became" a Jewish festival which in turn was taken over by the Christians as their spring celebration, some would have it that Easter is essentially a pagan rite for springtime.

Apart from the faulty logic in this reconstruction, and apart from its distortion of Palestinian climate, it fails to reckon adequately with the inveterate historical bias of ancient Israel. As Hans Joachim Kraus has well shown,[22] the Passover was thoroughly historicized long before the first century. By Jesus' day, the Pascha was the annual celebration of the greatest event in Jewish sacred history, the coming out of bondage in Egypt.

Thus when that Jewish Christian St. Paul wrote, "Christ our Passover is sacrificed for us: therefore let us keep the feast" (I Cor. 5:7), he was seeing in Christ's resurrection from the dead not a rebirth of fertility in the earth, but a new exodus from slavery into freedom. Since human bondage to death has deep parallels to the earth's bondage to winter, one can of course play on this concurrent symbolism. Our minds are lured irresistibly in this direction by Easter eggs and Easter bunnies and two thousand years of Christian poetry. But this connection remains, as Christians see it, an accidental one, in the ancient meaning of that word. The essential connection of Easter is with Jesus' resurrection. Its tie with spring flowers may not seem fortuitous in the northern temperate zone, but it is eminently clear to Easter worshipers in Melbourne, Santiago, and Capetown.[23]

Not until the fourth century did the whole Church have a festival in honor of their Lord's incarnation. The motives for developing one were intrinsic to the developing life and thought of the community. On the inner theologic of Christian faith, as Oscar Culmann has argued, it appears almost inevitable.[24] But celebrating a Feast of the Incarnation is not synonymous with commemorating Jesus' birthday. Indeed, no record of the day of his birth survived. By a variety of ingenious calculations, different Church Fathers came up with suggested dates in March, April and May; but they reached no agreement. The historical evidence suggests that Christians in Rome chose December 25 deliberately to combat the influence of the Feast of the Unconquered Sun on that day, and that this date gradually prevailed in the rest of the Church.

The Eastern Churches, however, have never made Christmas the equal to Epiphany, their original incarnation festival on January 6. Since the celebration of Epiphany probably started in Egypt, where January 6 was anciently the beginning of the winter solstice, again the link between Christian holidays and the movements of the sun is undeniable. But again it is apparent that only by disregarding the intentions of those who celebrate them can these two feasts be understood merely as human responses to biocosmic rhythms. Two other options for interpreting the meaning of these holiday seasons remain, however. Both the history of these feasts, and the ways they are understood by people who celebrate them today, indicate that they can be read with major reference to time past or, less simply, as evidence of things to come. These are similar to the options recognized in the first chapter as backward or forward looking, but in a very different guise. For whereas there a "historical" view of time appeared to open possibilities for the future and a "circular" view of time to be linked with ancient man's mystery rites, in this new context, those who see the Church's year as a mystery are those who stress its eschatological dimension oriented to what is yet to come. This new context also exposes another weakness in too simple antitheses in temporal thought. For it appears that, in concrete response to active participation in Christian holidays, the same human beings can give one stress to one occasion and its reputed opposite to another in the course of the same twelve months.

Consider again the two great festivals of Christmas and Easter. The former as we know it is a Western festival which invites worshipers to equate December 25 with the day Jesus was born. We seem to have here a prime example of looking backward to a baby in a manger in Bethlehem, a historical approach demonstrably popular in the West once fourth century Christians began journeying to the Holy Land. In clear contrast, Eastern Christians celebrate a Feast of Epiphany with maximum concern for the mystery of the Incarnation and minimal interest in whatever day of whatever month an infant was wrapped in swaddling clothes.

So far this bears out the stereotyped West-East antithesis in time concepts. But when one turns to Easter, the situation is reversed. Now the Easterners appear to insist on past-event precision and the Westerners to stress timeless mystery. For many years the second century Church was torn to the point of schism over the question of the date of Easter. Jewish chronology has given the name for this celebrated quarrel in church history, since for Jews Passover occurs on the 14th of Nisan, the quartodeciman day of the month.

Granting political and prideful mixed-motives in the Quartodeciman Controversy, the substantive issue was whether one should commemorate the Resurrection on the Passover (and hence with an eye on time past), or always on a Sunday (and hence with an eye on its recurring realization in the midst of the worshiping community). Christians in Asia Minor supported the first position; Christians in Rome, the second. As early as 154 or 155, the Bishop of Smyrna called on the Bishop of Rome to discuss the difference in the dates on which their respective churches were observing the Feast. For another thirty-five years the province of Asia continued to observe Easter on the 14th of Nisan, although Quartodecimans were condemned by other Christians as Judaizers.

Impatient as one may be with this seemingly trivial reason for schism in the Church, the intensity of feeling on the subject indicates again the depth of meaning people find in their own view of time. To challenge it is also to threaten an individual's or a community's identity. Without oversimplifying the complex historical picture,[25] I think we can see here another form of the eschatological tension in Christianity. A constant human desire to dissolve the tension appears to me to be evident in the Western view of Christmas (insofar as that is reflected in grottos and crèches) and in the Eastern view of Easter (insofar as that is reflected in fighting for the 14th of Nisan).

At least since the fourth century, the Church Year has invited men to think about the past and about the future. And at least since the fourth century some Christians have dissolved the tension by choosing what might well be called a tourist's view of time, while others have elected to affirm it through their understanding of mystery in holidays.

Classic examples of the tourist view of the Christian year are provided by the Spanish nun Etheria, who visited the Holy Land about 395,[26] and by the latterday Scottish clergyman, A. Allan McArthur, who in effect takes her pilgrimage again in the interests of reintroducing the Church Year into the Church of Scotland, which alone of all the Reformation churches formally abandoned it.[27]

Etheria's account of her visit to Jerusalem in the late fourth century is packed with details of when and where Christians worshiped in that Holy City. It conveys such a vivid sense of goings and comings in observance of Epiphany and Easter that one wants to retain the flavor of the document by using its Latin title, *Peregrinatio Etheriae*. The author is a woman who would come home today not just with colored slides but with motion pictures of her trip.

She pictures the celebration of Epiphany as a joyful eight

day round of revisiting the places where Jesus was born and suffered and died and rose again. The resident monks, she acknowledges, keep vigil in the church in Bethlehem throughout the octave; but after a nighttime service there, the Bishop leads a procession on foot back to Jerusalem. Arriving a little before daybreak, the whole crowd goes to pray at the Church of the Resurrection, where they find a great number of lights already ablaze. Then, after what must have been a very short rest, everyone reassembles at Golgotha for Mass, with lessons and hymns and sermons all appropriate to the day.

Etheria's faithful record, first published in the late nineteenth century, is a mine of information for liturgical scholars. Our interest at the moment is in the attitude toward the Church Year which it typifies. When one returns from Jerusalem to Rome or Florence or Toledo, one finds from the time of Etheria to the present a growing tendency to consider the Church calendar as an annual pilgrimage into the past, with appropriate stops at all the spots where Jesus did memorable things. Thus the new interest in holy places, which tradition says was started by the Emperor Constantine's mother, is gradually assimilated by holy times. This is a dislocation of that Church Year which developed in Jesus' homeland.

Essentially the same tourist attitude toward this round of Christian holidays informs the work of one of Etheria's modern admirers. At the conclusion of his careful and capable review of the Church Year, still a major source of information about the details of its evolution, A. Allan McArthur asks, "What attitude do we adopt to this pattern?" [28] Having acknowledged the need for a choice here, he presents his own: "We must endeavor to apply the Jerusalem insight more fully, so that the Life of our Lord may be more evident in the Year." [29]

Contemporary Christians who choose this option may adopt a rational, educational view of the Church Year—one comparable to Sheldon's *In His Steps*. Or they may conceive it in more mystical terms—comparable to Thomas à Kempis's *Imitation of Christ*. In either case, the historical approach offers a chance to relive in microcosm each twelve months what

Jesus himself experienced in his thirty-some years. By walking in his footsteps one imitates his rhythms. By celebrating Christmas, this view suggests, Christians can now join the shepherds at Bethlehem. Even though they cannot be at the alleged site of the Holy Sepulchre on Easter, as Etheria was, they can go each year while it is yet dark to a Sunrise Service. Through the year they can participate imaginatively in all the decisive events recounted in the New Testament.

An alternative attitude toward the annual round of Christian feasts offers Christians a chance instead to experience the full mystery of God's plan for mankind, not only in each Eucharist but also in each full cycle of Christian holidays. The stress in this interpretation is on times and seasons wherein Christian worshipers encounter the power of the Holy Spirit to make present that which has already happened and which is yet to come.

One modern spokesman for this option, the Oratorian Louis Bouyer, finds warrant for his understanding of "the mystery of the liturgical year" in Church Fathers both East and West. He cites persuasive passages from homilies of St. Gregory Nazianzus and of Pope Leo the Great to show that "in the liturgical year we are not only making a commemoration of the past but also actually living again the realities on which we are meditating with the Church." [30]

Bouyer explores directly the question of what relationship exists between "that cyclical time in which nature operates and causes man to operate, and that irreversible historic time in which God has intervened once and for all and brought about a decisive change in man and in the whole human world." [31] His answer to this question is weighted heavily toward a nature-centered and hence cyclical experience of time which we have suggested is no longer a decisive one for most men today. But Bouyer does not stop there. He goes on to change his image of time from a circle to a spiral, and thus to suggest a new way of conceiving the annual rhythms: "The divine intervention in history obviously did not suddenly put a stop to its natural rhythms. If it had done so, it would have only suppressed human history. . . . What the divine intervention does, therefore, is to open up, as it were, those closed cycles of time, which up to that moment had been only revolving on themselves. These cycles . . . are now in a process of development into a larger and larger spiral, and this process will reach its term at the moment when the spiral of human history loses itself, or rather, finds its fulfillment in God's eternity." [32]

Bouyer's exposition of the mystery theme centers notably on the two major feasts which we have so far made central also (partly because they are best known), Christmas-Epiphany and Easter. It does not stress the third major festival of the Christian year, the Feast of Pentecost. In this respect, it represents a dated approach of the mid-fifties, one already significantly changing under the impact of ecumenical thought and new historical evidence. A more recent summary of the liturgical year sets the wider focus which leads to a different understanding of the whole sequence: the year "revolves around the three primary feasts of Easter and Pentecost, which go back to apostolic times, and Christmas-Epiphany, instituted in the fourth century." [33]

Starting from this triple framework, Massey Shepherd's 1965 development of the mystery theme is significantly different from Bouyer's. "The Christian year," Shepherd writes as Bouyer might have, "is a mystery through which every moment and all times and seasons of this life are transcended and fulfilled in that reality which is beyond time." [34] But he goes on then to divide the year into two halves, from Advent to Pentecost and from Pentecost to Advent. The first half moves, in this interpretation, to the climax of the outpouring of the Holy Spirit fifty days after Easter. The second half moves from Pentecost (understood as the decisive dividing point in human history) toward the final Advent and Epiphany. The Church Year so interpreted is a reflection of the Church's experience of itself as living between the Ages.

The eschatological mystery is precisely stated: "In actual chronological time, we are living today—in this year of grace

1965—between the first Pentecost and the last Advent. But in the mystery of existence in the Christian transcendence and transfiguration of time, we live in the totality of all that is encompassed between first Advent and Epiphany and final Advent and Epiphany. . . . The Christian Year, however, makes present to us here and now all that is final and ultimate. The liturgy is not a discipline that prepares us step by step for some future goal and reward. The liturgy is at any time and in any place that goal present and real *now*." [35] It is essential to reread such a compact paragraph in order to absorb its full ambiguity. In "actual" time we are living between the times. But in the liturgy, the *eschaton* is now.

Such an exposition perceives, as it were, two New Year's seasons in each round of holidays. It turns attention decisively beyond both past and present toward the coming of the Kingdom; but without postponing that Coming by a simple futurist view of the End.

The double focus of Advent here suggested is found in the scripture readings and hymns which the Church has long used in this season of preparation for the coming of the Lord. The polarity of the season finds poetic expression in the familiar Advent hymn, "O Come, O Come Emmanuel," a metrical version of the seven great antiphons which for centuries have been part of the Advent liturgy. The Coming One so urgently invited and so tensely awaited is not merely a baby in Bethlehem but Creator and Judge, King and Saviour whose next epiphany, the New Testament says, will be in power and great glory. Christian worshipers today give assent to this New Testament belief each time they recite the Lord's Prayer or one of the historic Creeds. Their concomitant response is expressed in a section of Paul's letter to the Romans long read in the Advent season: "May the God of hope fill you with all joy and peace in believing, that you may abound in hope, through the power of the Holy Spirit" (15:13).

Finally we come to age sixty-five and retirement. In anticipation, this major turning point in modern life appears to many as the end of the round of weekends and holidays, the goal imparting its meaning to the whole. When it arrives, it comes to many as a traumatic crisis with serious consequences for mental health.

Anthropologists have long recognized that all men everywhere cope ceremonially with the crises in their individual life cycles. Since publication in 1908 of Arnold van Gennep's analysis of ritual behavior, *Rites de Passage,* his title has become a standard term for this social fact. In the introduction to a 1961 paperback reissue of this classic study, Solon T. Kimball observes that "there is no evidence that a secularized world has lessened the need for ritualized expression of an individual's transition from one status to another." [36]

The New York Times has documented Kimball's comment with a report from Moscow describing solemn civil rites which Soviet ideologists were devising for major events in people's personal lives, in order to "wean them away from religious influences." [37] Along with birth and marriage, the Communist list of critical occasions includes the first day of school, the delivery of an internal passport to sixteen-year-olds, induction into the army, and starting in the first job. There is no mention of ending that job with a testimonial dinner and an engraved watch.

Christians also have developed their rites to mark in various ways the cycle of life from birth to death. Similarities have often been noted between Christian practices of confirmation and the puberty rites of other cultures. So, too, in the case of marriage and burial customs. In the Christian community, however, the major rite of passage is undoubtedly baptism, almost universally considered an essential element of Christian worship. Christian worshipers find, in their understanding of this rite, an alternative to retirement as the goal and end of their working years. Their very quarrels over its proper performance and significance testify to their sense of its importance in the Christian way of being-toward-death.

Considerable evidence from the early Church shows that for centuries baptism was a complex, dramatic act of initiation.[38] It was usually performed only once a year at Easter.

To be eligible, a man or woman enrolled first as a catechumen, and underwent a three year period of instruction and testing. During this period he was not permitted to pray with the "faithful"; that is, to share in the intercessions with those already initiated. At the end of three years, his sponsors had to testify that he had lived piously as a catechumen and "filled every good work."

If a man passed this examination, he was advanced to the status of a candidate for baptism and began an even more rigorous period of preparation, one which included daily exorcisms and culminated in a two day fast topped by a full night's vigil. At dawn on Easter, he then entered the baptistry adjoining the church, stripped completely, and went down naked into the water. Women were instructed to remove even their rings and hairpins, so that literally nothing was carried over from the past life.

Prior to submerging, the candidate was anointed with oil from head to toe, and required to abjure Satan and all his works. In the water, between drownings as it were, he thrice pledged his faith in God—Father, Son, and Holy Spirit. Emerging from the pool he was again anointed, and in some communities at least, given a new white robe to wear. Then he was led with the other newly baptized into the midst of the assembly of waiting Christians, presented to the bishop for the laying on of hands and yet another sealing with oil and the sign of the cross. Then—for the first time—he immediately participated in the celebration of the Easter Eucharist which completed his initiation into the holy mysteries.

The dramatic impact of such an experience after such intense preparation must have been great. On these grounds at least, one must regard as a loss the fact that adult baptism by immersion ceased to be the norm of Christian initiation in the Church as a whole, to be replaced by sprinkling a few drops of water on a baby's head. The Reformation groups which refused to baptize infants, however, and their successors in the Baptist tradition today, do not rest their case for believers baptism on the liturgical practices of the second to fourth centuries. They insist that adults show forth their faith in Christ prior to baptism because they believe this to be the norm of the New Testament. Beyond a doubt, as it seems to me, the New Testament understanding of baptism is expressed in and evoked by the liturgical act which has just been described.

The rich symbolism of the ancient initiation rite, it is true, offers almost limitless material for interpreting its meaning, as many lectures and sermons from the patristic period prove. But one theme is constant: to experience baptism is to experience death and resurrection; it is a *transitus* through death to new life in Christ. This interpretation is explicit in Paul's letter to the Romans when he asks: "Do you not know that all of us who have been baptized into Christ Jesus were baptized into his death? We were buried therefore with him by baptism into death, so that as Christ was raised from the dead by the glory of the Father, we too might walk in newness of life" (6:3–4).

Just after Easter about the year 350, Cyril, Bishop of Jerusalem, read that whole Romans passage before his second lecture to a group of newly baptized Christians still under instruction, explaining further what they had recently been through. He reminds them that, by stripping, they have put off the old man with his deeds. They are now reborn for new deeds. He tries to explain the temporal paradox by quoting from Ecclesiastes, "a time to be born and a time to die." "But in your case," he says, "the reverse is true: a time to die and a time to be born. In fact, a single time accomplished both. . . ." [39]

Using many of the same biblical texts with which Cyril's lectures bristle, a modern New Testament scholar, Ernst Käsemann, interprets baptism with a similar emphasis on its ethical dimension of walking in newness of life. Käsemann acknowledges the general mythological background of the death and rebirth theme in Christian initiation, but he insists that it nevertheless becomes something radically different in Christian practice. His understanding of this rite of passage reflects again the contemporary stress on Christian eschatology, and shows why Christian worshipers may choose baptism rather than retirement as the major turning point to give meaning to all of life.

For Christianity as for other religions, Käsemann says, "true existence" really means "Here is a being determined by a particular sphere of influence." In baptism, as he sees it, "the Christian changes from one jurisdiction to another." Members of the Christian community lose their old form of existence; they are translated through baptism into a new one. Using more traditional language, he repeats the same idea: "They make the successful journey from the power of darkness into the kingdom of God's dear Son. . . ." [40]

Because this journey has brought the believer into immediate relationship with Christ and the community which is called his Body, the old powers have no more control over him. But, and here is where Käsemann introduces that tension which distinguishes Christian experience from an all's-right-with-the-world complacency, the Kingdom of the Son must be understood as an eschatological one: "The community is his body inasmuch as it lives from the resurrection of the dead and marches toward the resurrection of the dead. But that means, in the here and now, that it stands within the forgiveness of sins. It neither means, nor indeed can mean, anything else at all. Because it stands within forgiveness, it is a new creation." [41]

In their views on weekends and holidays, as well as in the way they view their initiation into the worshiping community, we have said in this chapter, Christians constantly express a sense of living already in a new creation. But they are also convinced that they are marching through time toward that new creation of which they experience only a foretaste in their worship. They live with the rhythmic tension of the future present and march to its beat.

Chapter 4

SPEAKING AND HEARING

SPEAKING AND HEARING are constant activities in almost all worship. In this chapter we will consider the four ways in which these two phenomena manifest themselves most prominently in Christian worship. In their services most Christians read or listen to readings from the Bible; they preach or listen to preaching related to that reading; they respond in some form of sung praise; they open their mouths in prayer. These are the elements of Christian worship identified in the first chapter as inherited from the synagogue and elaborated into the Ministry of the Word.

Today the speaking and hearing of worship appear to be poised between two cultural forces. The first offers grounds for optimism among those who are worried about the future of worship, since we may have entered a new auditory age wherein words can again be proclaimed and heard. The other raises serious doubts as to whether Christian worship can any longer speak to people no matter how new-minted the words it uses, since every language of faith may be too near death.

Speaking for the optimistic side is that irritating *agent provocateur,* Marshall McLuhan, who must nevertheless be hailed as a molder of the present mood. His most important nonbook, *The Gutenberg Galaxy,* interlards its pronouncements of "majestic simple-mindedness" [1] with insights no contemporary student of worship can ignore. The work is a deliberate mosaic of quotations around the central theme of the new sensory interplay which these post-literate, electronic times demand and enforce. If McLuhan has correctly diagnosed the changed modes of awareness created by the new electromagnetic world, we are already in a period when men can once more become deeply involved in the speaking and hearing of worship.

McLuhan's basic thesis in *The Gutenberg Galaxy* is that the phonetic alphabet and the printing press together conspired to imprison men in a world tyrannized by visual, linear perception. Well into the "scribal" culture of the late Middle Ages, he argues, man was still open to "the magical world of the ear," a world charged with drama and emotion, a world loaded with direct personal significance for the hearer. With the advent of television and computer, he thinks, our world is translating itself back into an oral and auditory world, into a culture of electric all-at-onceness.[2] "Consistently, the twentieth century has worked to free itself," he concludes, "from the conditions of passivity, which is to say, from the Gutenberg heritage itself."[3] And so our "newspaper somnambulism" can give way to "a kind of witty jazz."[4]

The prospect which McLuhan conjures up of electronic man united in his global village is not without its terrors. Indeed terror, he insists, "is the normal state of any oral society."[5] Sounds are known there as dynamic things; they speak to men of movement in the bush; they put him on the alert. But they also bring "the collective dimension of human experience fully into the conscious wake-a-day world,"[6] just as the new electric technology has already managed to do through television.

Even if McLuhan's kaleidoscope had not stopped briefly at the liturgical renewal, represented by excerpts from Louis Bouyer's book which we introduced above, the implications of his thinking for contemporary worship would be inescapable. In another essay, he acknowledges his debt to T. S. Eliot's concept of the auditory imagination. Eliot described this as "the feeling for syllable and rhythm, penetrating far below the conscious levels of thought and feeling, invigorating every

word . . . seeking the beginning and the end." [7] McLuhan
has captured the same human potentiality in his phrase, "a
return to the Africa within." [8]

McLuhan's drum beats a message of hope for the oral-audi-
tory of worship, but it has not yet drowned the voices of those
who say it comes too late. Modern man has grown completely
tone deaf, these prophets of gloom believe; he can no longer
hear religious language. The problem could not be posed more
sharply than by D. H. Lawrence: "I just was never able to
understand the language of salvation. . . . When the evangeli-
cal says: Behold the Lamb of God! what on earth does he
want one to behold? Are we invited to look at a lamb, with
woolly, muttony appearance?" [9] It is intriguing to note that
Lawrence here betrays precisely that tyranny of visual perception which McLuhan blames on the Gutenberg galaxy
and whose overthrow he heralds. Yet the dilemma is too widely
shared to be dismissed. Church language, Krister Stendahl
once remarked, is a kind of Yiddish, a language which is
heart-warming in the Ghetto but totally useless for communicating to the outside world. As we listen to some of the ways
in which Christian worship encourages "the live friction of
voice and ear," [10] we will try to continue to hear this charge.

Hearing the Word of God was a central theme of the Protestant Reformation. In the sixteenth century this meant much
more than a simple "Back to the Bible!" campaign, but such
a campaign was included. Martin Luther viewed coming together to hear God's word as a central purpose of Christian
worship. Less than a century after Johann Gutenberg had
invented printing from movable type, Luther's vernacular
translation of the New Testament was ready for the new
presses. For the first time German farmers and housewives
were able to hear that Word in the same earthy language they
used every day in the kitchen and the marketplace.

The German Mass did not remove the sacred aura which
surrounded the public reading of Scripture, however. A modern reader, who has at least a five-foot bookshelf somewhere
in his house, must make a major act of will to imagine the

procedure and power of such reading before books became the birthright of everyman. Eric Werner recalls the high solemnity in ancient times when representatives of an esoteric caste of priests ceremoniously exposed their scrolls or cuneiform tablets before an illiterate throng, chanted a portion of the sacred text in ancient modes, and then removed them from the rude gaze of ordinary men.[11] No such cult readings, Werner and others believe, can be exempted from the theory that a major function of religious language is theurgic, that it is a kind of magic to manipulate the sacred powers of the universe with holy sound.

Certainly Jews continued for centuries to chant their sacred texts according to rigid rules of tone and accent; and certainly the Christians, as we have seen, took over some of their solemn customs surrounding the readings, including Hebrew chant forms. Some parts of the church continued to read from both the Law and the Prophets, and added new Christian texts as well, so that (in the Syrian liturgy, for example) there could be as many as six selections read. In other parts of the church three appointed readings became the norm, including one from the Old Testament and ending always with a selection from the Gospels. Gradually the idea of two predominated in the West, with the understanding that the first one might be from the Old Testament instead of from an apostolic "epistle" as such.

For centuries, of course, this meant that more than one manuscript was needed; and customs elaborated decreeing who might read which, where, and how. Beginning from the fifth century in the West, the right to read from the Gospel, the *verba Verbi,* was reserved to the deacon. By the tenth century that book was solemnly delivered into his hands as part of his ordination ceremony. In the later Middle Ages the only known exception to this rule that only deacons read the Gospel was the Emperor himself, who was allowed to sing the Gospel at midnight Mass on Christmas.[12]

The special honor paid to the book from which the Gospel was read, and the manner of its reading were related in Christian understanding to the idea that the Gospel is "the mouth of Christ," as Augustine phrased it.[13] Martin Luther voices an old idea when he says that Christians gather for worship in order that "our dear Lord Himself may speak to us through His Holy Word." [14] Such an idea of the Word led to and followed from a whole cluster of ceremonies: carrying the Book in procession; chanting it from a special spot; standing to listen to its words; sandwiching its reading between special salutations of prayer and praise. This same attitude toward the Book appears today in those Protestant churches which play a special beam of light on an open Bible left lying on the Communion table.

What the Reformers insisted on, however, was that the words must be heard and understood. And so ministers were directed to read in the vernacular and in a loud clear tone. But Reformation man, it should be remembered, still lived in what McLuhan calls a manuscript culture. He had not yet suffered that atrophy of the ear which makes it so difficult for literate man in the Western world to hear the Word of God through listening once a week to a short paragraph or two read aloud from a book he has a copy of at home.

Throughout the Middle Ages as in antiquity, reading was accomplished not principally with the eyes, but, as Dom Jean Leclercq has vividly described it, "with the lips, pronouncing what they saw, and with the ears, listening to the words pronounced, hearing what is called the 'voices of the pages.' It is a real acoustical reading; *legere* means at the same time *audire*. . . ." [15] Leclercq claims that doctors even used to recommend reading to their patients as a physical exercise equivalent to jogging.

For St. Benedict or St. Augustine the whole concept of *lectio* still meant "an activity which, like chant and writing, requires the participation of the whole body and the whole mind." [16] Some of this sense of the reading-hearing activity, at least, was still alive in the sixteenth century. If typographic man does not read in the same way, no more is he able to hear and remember what is read to him.

Some of the Reformers wanted to restore again the old idea of a *lectio continua* whereby the whole Bible would be read aloud in order. The early Church had used two principles in ordering readings for public worship—choosing both sequences from the same book of the Bible, and selections fitting the seasons of the church year. The oldest surviving lectionaries in the Roman Church show a combination of the two in the "epistles" and gospels appointed for Sunday Eucharists.

The year's reading thus rehearsed before the people only part of the biblical story. Furthermore, the daily office as it had developed in the Middle Ages included many extra-biblical readings from lives of martyrs and saints and from sermons by the Fathers. The sixteenth century Protestants repudiated completely the public reading of the latter. Many of them also abandoned the old Sunday lectionary completely. In its place the Westminster Assembly in 1645, for example, directed that the canonical books should be read straight through in sequence, one chapter from the Old and one from the New Testament at each meeting for public worship, until the whole Bible had been read. Man's capacity to listen to reading aloud was evidently still greater in the seventeenth century than in the twentieth. In their new revisions of the liturgy today, however, Presbyterians as well as Lutherans, Methodists, and Episcopalians all provide lectionaries related to the Church Year, and related to some extent to the old Roman Eucharistic lectionary.[17]

Not all Protestant parishes follow a lectionary in their normal Sunday services, to be sure; but those who do believe it protects both congregation and preacher from personal whims and passing fancies. Only waning authority of the lectionary, as one Lutheran put it recently, has enabled the Protestant clergy "to exercise so bland a selectivity within the corpus of the New Testament utterances."[18] Simply because he isn't struck by Luke 21:25–36 on the Second Sunday in Advent, the preacher is "not thereby released from the thundering New Testament words about the signs of the time. . . ."[19]

"Here shall follow the sermon." Although not all would

use the imperative words of this old rubric, all churches affected by liturgical renewal are agreed that preaching is an essential part of the Service of the Word, and therefore to be understood in the context of the action of the People of God. Awkward efforts to introduce something called the dialogue sermon reflect this desire to recover a dynamic sense of congregational participation in what had become perhaps the most passive period in Christian worship. Such a frontal attack appears to overlook the fact that listening can itself be an active role.

Contemporary writing about sermons, most of it by and for preachers, makes at best a passing acknowledgment that the congregation has any role to play. Thus congregations appear still to sit back thinking of themselves as a captive audience, as if they associated the act of *granting* an audience only with popes and kings. Both phrases reveal the degree to which we have lost an active sense of our ears.

The sermon, nevertheless, remains the occasion when the preacher proclaims and the other worshipers respond to the Word of God. In the majority of Christian churches the people are not invited to express that response overtly until the sermon is finished. Although some congregations retain the custom of vocal responses such as Amen! in the course of preaching, many other congregations do not feel free even to smile, much less give any audible response to the preached Word. Fashions in listening change as much as fashions in speaking.

When the sermon is thought of in the context of the total liturgy instead of as "the holy branch office of the local psychiatric clinic," [20] it raises new problems about its purpose. In his contribution to the recent series "Ecumenical Studies in Worship," von Allmen—rightly claiming that the Reformed Church has much to contribute to the ecumenical movement in the matter of preaching—distinguishes two essential types: the missionary sermon, which has its parallel with the sacrament of Baptism; and the up-building sermon, which has its parallel with the sacrament of the Lord's Supper. The purpose of the latter is captured in a beautifully auditory image—"to make the Gospel resound in the church." [21] In an article on "The Liturgy of the Word," published not long afterwards, the Roman Catholic George Tavard draws a similar distinction.[22]

Both men agree that the dominant need in a sermon in the context of the Eucharist is not mere "relevance" but rather "disturbance." Really faithful preaching of the Word is risky for all concerned. Its function is to open up the faithful. Preaching is part of "an eschatological event."

The eschatological purpose and context of the sermon also sound powerfully in Joseph Sittler's distinguished lectures on preaching: "The Christian life," he says, "is drawn taut between the Amen and the Come. This tautness has its suffering, its waiting, and its peculiar service to the world. . . . Christian worship has been the strange music of these taut and joyous lives in history. . . ." [23] With this understanding of worship, Sittler offers two very important insights for our inquiry into the dynamics of speaking and hearing the Word of God through the sermon, and suggests thereby a partial answer to the language problems of a D. H. Lawrence.

In the environment of the worshiping community there are mutual relationships among the language of the sermon, the language of the scripture readings which precede it, and the prayers and other actions which follow it. The sermon thus is not to be considered in isolation from its liturgical matrix. Current linguistic theory tells us that one learns a language not by learning the meanings of words but as a way of feeling and exploring his environment.[25] Insofar as the worshiper to whom the Word of God is addressed in the sermon is actively involved in exploring the whole environment where this language is used, he may thereby learn the language more native to the preacher.

The second suggestion from Sittler's profoundly stimulating book has to do with the role of imagination. Sittler devoted two of his five lectures for prospective preachers to the subject of imagination. Images, and along with them man's image-making powers, form a subject to which we will return in Part II, where we will be concerned with the ways we shape our space. The need to recognize them here reminds us that all our perception is multisensory. It makes sense to say that we listen with the mind's eye.

Imagination is essential for the preacher, Sittler has said with care, because it is a way of discovering hitherto unseen relationships between things.[26] For the man in the pew, one might add, it is also a way of discovering hitherto unheard of relationships between things. Our imaginative powers, as Coleridge long ago noted, are modes of energy. If the man who preaches and the man who listens are both to hear the Word of God addressed to them in this time of worship between the Ages, both must expend energy. Those who audit sermons might well note the energy implicit in the new images of the electric age which speak of being turned off—and on.

Two of the most energetically turned-on men the Christian Church has ever known are John and Charles Wesley. Moving strenuously about Britain and her colonies, they taught people how to respond to the preached Word with the language of song. Through their *Collection of Hymns for the Use of the People Called Methodists,* they contributed so much to all subsequent Christian worship that one turns naturally to Methodism for help in thinking about this language of faith.

Singing is, of course, a mode of speaking and hearing omnipresent in Christian worship. Histories of hymnody are compelled to begin with the psalms of Israel, if not with that dawn of Creation when the morning stars sang together and all the sons of God shouted for joy. Not only the familiar canticles from St. Luke's Gospel, but snatches of other Christian hymns scattered throughout the New Testament prove that Christians have always been a singing people. In recent years we have learned to recognize how deeply that activity has influenced both the form and content of the Church's scripture. What people believe has always been partly the result of what they do, much as we still like to think of it the other way around. For almost two thousand years Christians have continued to sing such great hymns as the *Gloria in Excelsis* and the *Sanctus,* which early unfolded out of biblical song. For almost two thousand years they have burst into new song in response to new experience. That apocryphal story of Ambrose and Augustine composing the *Te Deum* in antiphonal joy at the moment of Augustine's baptism is, in that sense, a true story of the Lord's song in strange lands. So, in the same sense, is the legend of St. Patrick warding off enemies by chanting the strong name of Christ. The Wesleys were not the first to discover the magic powers of singing.

Nor were they the first to use song in conscious appeal to the minds and hearts of men. Martin Luther set about making "German psalms" for the people in order that the Word of God might be "kept alive among them by singing." [27] John Calvin imported a musician from Paris not only to compose psalm tunes of fitting dignity to be sung in church, but also to teach them first to children so that their parents in turn would be more effectively instructed.[28] In the same spirit John Wesley collected, translated, and published hymns he thought of as a "body of experimental and practical divinity." [29]

But it is a mistake to imply that any of these men is only a propagandist using music as a device to instill scripture lessons, or to play upon the emotions of hitherto impenitent sinners. All of them were convinced that the heart of worship is praise of God and that vocal music is man's God-given instrument for praising.

With Methodism's vital upsurge of song in the eighteenth century, moreover, we hear again those Dionysian currents which Nietzsche associated with all creative revolutions. When one reads accounts of Charles Wesley leaping from his horse to jot down by the roadside new ideas for one of his 6500 hymns, he appears unmistakably as a kind of Dionysian knight of faith. Against such energy, the Establishment's charge of enthusiast must be turned back to its radical sense. He was indeed *en theos*. Or, to borrow McLuhan's language again, he was engaged in opening up the eighteenth century version of newspaper somnambulism to the eighteenth century version of a witty jazz.

This is a man, as Erik Routley notes, who rarely omits the

idea of freedom from a hymn, whatever its subject.[30] "O for 1000 tongues to sing," the song he wrote on May 21, 1739, the first anniversary of his conversion, is an outburst of joyous energy. Because Charles Wesley's loosened tongue did not stop praising the glories of his God and King, all Christian worship has been enriched.

The index of the 1904 English edition of the Methodist hymnal carried the simple line, "Where no name is given it may be assumed that the hymn is the work of Mr. Charles Wesley." [31] Fifty-four of his hymns were in the last Methodist hymnal in America. But the words of Wesley's praise have become part of all English language hymnody: "Hark! the herald angels sing," "Christ the Lord is risen today," "Love divine, all loves excelling," "Christ whose glory fills the sky"— these first lines alone are enough to show what an indelible mark Wesley has left on the Christian viscera.

Over and above Charles Wesley's personal gift to Christian worship, and over and above Methodism's peculiar honors to their King (to use Isaac Watts' equivalent for the phrase "contribution to the ecumenical church"), three aspects of his hymnody deserve comment in relation to singing worship in general.

First, Charles Wesley, more than his predecessor Isaac Watts or half a dozen other great writers of English hymns one could name, is open to charges of sentimentality and of individualism. He is often criticized for writing too much in the first person singular. Zinzendorf's pietism and William Law's mysticism, it is objected, are both antithetical to the objective praise of God proper to corporate worship; and traces of both of them are apparent in such a hymn as "Jesu, lover of my soul."

In response to this kind of criticism, Erik Routley has produced one packed sentence which speaks volumes about the dynamics of hymnody: "There is no explaining the mystery which makes the Church gather together to sing such intimate lines as these, as though the whole singing company were a single singing person." [32] I read this sentence to mean that the hymns of a Wesley refute all the old antitheses between individual and corporate worship. They prove that matters are much more complicated than that. What a man does in his solitude speaks to all of his fellows gathered in worship; what happens in the gathering is experienced not as a denial but as a deepening of his own unique selfhood. Routley is not just telling us what everyone knows—that a good rousing song binds a group together. He is speaking out of the Christian worshiper's experience that he is more himself the more he is part of that whole.

Second, Methodist hymnody has welded Charles Wesley's words to unforgettable tunes. The point could be made most simply if you would just whistle your favorite hymn tune. The words, as the Wesleys well knew, are latent in that tune. Bernard Manning has written eloquently of the way in which in wartime simply hearing the familiar tunes of Wesley's hymns reassured him of "the unshaken truth of essential Christianity." [33] Although he readily admits that any "fifth-rate psychologist" could offer an explanation for this, he is not ready to accept that explanation as the whole story.

As one not-unprejudiced commentator rather quaintly explains: "It was natural that the Methodists, being democratic and of the people, should have relied upon tunes of the folk style." [34] Because Charles Wesley wrote his hymns without regard for established modes of sacred music, they were free to be attached to the meters and rhythms of secular melodies. Especially in the camp meeting on the American frontier, some of them came to be fused permanently with tunes which are sometimes the despair of musical purists. But whatever its aesthetic consequences, this fusion of words with tunes is analogous, it seems to me, to what happens to persons through the singing of hymns in worship. What Routley has said apropos of the word "praise" in all languages well expresses it: "they exercise the muscles of the mouth and throat, and the strength of piety to the utmost." [35]

Finally, and here I am again indebted to suggestions from the British hymnologist, Charles Wesley's hymns are scriptural hymns; and this means that they invite us into a theatre of tension. It is easy to miss this note. We can lull ourselves with good old gospel hymns as much as we are lulled by insidious jingles telling us what toothpaste to buy. But if one looks twice at Wesley's words, as Routley insists that we do, it is suddenly loud and clear that he too was hung up between the already and the not-yet. He gives worshipers words with which to invite their future into the present moment of worship.

In the Advent hymns "Come, thou long expected Jesus" and "Lo! he comes, with clouds descending," the point is self-evident. In "Christ whose glory fills the sky," it is less obvious until one marks the way in which the writer has linked the metaphor "dayspring" from the subversive *Benedictus* (Luke 1:78) with the rare figure of speech "Sun of righteousness," from the prophet Malachi (4:2). The result is a reinforced expectancy as great as Paul's "the night is far gone, the day is at hand . . ." (Rom. 13:12). In "Love divine, all loves excelling," the invitation of the first verse, "Visit us . . ." is intensified in phrases of the second and third verses: "Come, almighty . . ."; "Suddenly return . . ."; "Finish then thy new creation. . . ."

Wesley believed that the Lord had already come and over-turned his personal life. He is a classic twice-born man. But his hymns praise also the Lord who is yet to come to set his people free. As Christians respond in such taut terms to the proclamation of the Word of God, they move with the New Testament community under the imperative to wake from sleep.

Noise wakes people up. Wide awake people make noise. Christians inherited a command to make a joyful noise unto the Lord. The words of the *Te Deum* they sing claim that angels and all the powers of heaven cry aloud in praise to God. At about the time that *Te Deum* was written, St. Jerome was able to describe worship in the Roman basilicas as a very noisy affair. The Amen of the people, he says, "resounded like heavenly thunder." [36] Nothing in the central tradition of Christian worship appears to account for the tiptoe and hushed whisper which many middle-class Americans reserve for churches and funeral parlors.

As we turn to think about the fourth form of speaking and hearing most common in Christian worship, vocal prayer, we encounter man's curious tendency to distinguish holy and unholy noises. Some worshipers appear to think that God can only hear pipe organs. Others appear to believe that effective prayer must be uttered in hollow tones reserved for Sunday mornings. With equal intensity other worshipers seem to think that Jesus runs with them only if he is greeted as casually as one would greet a barroom acquaintance. Christians still share the conviction of Vedic priests that the quality as well as the quantity of sound is critical in matters of worship. Why?

From the phenomenological perspective, making noise and going out of oneself toward another are reciprocally interrelated. Merleau-Ponty, for example, interprets loss of speech (in the clinical sense of aphasia) as a refusal of coexistence,[37] whereas participating in communal life is understood as prerequisite to learning a language. The latter point is clear when one considers what six weeks in Mexico can do for one's Spanish. Furthermore the spoken word appears to be a genuine gesture, sharing the same potentiality as the other gestures we have previously considered. Speech, that is, accomplishes thought. Students and teachers know this very well. They have all been surprised to discover what they "really" think in the process of saying it. The vigorous spoken word thus invigorates the speakers. Opening mouths opens persons toward the one to whom they speak.

If one tries to apply such ideas to that vastly complex subject of spoken prayer manifest in public worship, both the speaking persons and the speaking words claim attention. Three patterns of sharing the speaking role seem to be characteristic of church services. In churches as elsewhere the human propensity for electing a spokesman is evident; let the minister's voice be heard. Ever since Paul's dictum that things must be done decently and in order, the human propensity for all talking at once has been quelled in most churches, in favor of the ordered Apollonian practice of reciting certain prayers in unison. The mode of speaking truly indigenous to worship, however, is dialogic. Public prayer is first cousin of antiphonal singing.

Both the pattern and the intent of such an exchanged energy of prayer are well illustrated in the ancient liturgical greetings and responses widely used today, such as "The Lord be with you . . . And with you also." The alternating current of voice answering voice is still audible in translations of the hymn *Kyrie eleison,* perhaps especially when it is spoken responsively, "Lord have mercy . . . Christ have mercy." In the ancient Greek liturgies, the *Kyrie* was part of that form of prayer called a litany. The deacon announced intentions for which people were to pray, and the people responded each time, "Kyrie eleison." When the litany form of prayer was imported to the West, the Greek response came too. Well beyond the sixth century, it was still the people's part to cry out "Kyrie eleison!" [38]

The uses of the word "Amen" in Christian prayer, however, provide perhaps the best illustration of this responsive pattern, with its lively friction of voice and ear. About the year 150 Justin explains that the person who presides at Sunday morning worship offers up prayers and thanksgivings to the best of his ability, "and the people express their approval by saying *Amen*." [39] What that approval means is not conveyed by being told that *Amen* is an ancient Hebrew word for "So be it," nor by learning that where Jesus says "Verily, verily" in the King James version and "surely" or "truly" in modern translations, the Greek text has "Amen, Amen." The word comes alive only when one hears the thunder in the Roman basilicas, or Spanish congregations crying out *Amen* five times after each of the petitions of the Lord's Prayer, or the Copts crying *Amen* after each phrase the priest recites in the consecration prayer and finally shouting: "We believe and testify and give praise!" [40] Once again, the affirmation of the people is accomplished in the utterance of the people.

In prayerful response to the Word of God, then, it is the

speaking word not just the spoken word which has power. Truth, it has been well said, is carried alive into the heart by passion. "I-Thou," as Buber insisted, can only be spoken with the whole being. Both statements are also reminders that the more-than-cognitive language of prayer is always metaphoric. And metaphor, as poets recognize, is "the natural language of tension, of excitement, because it enables a man by a compressed violence of expression to rise to the level of the violent situation which provokes it." [41] Thy kingdom come! The Lord who taught his disciples to use this metaphor in prayer, Christians believe, was also one who healed the deaf and caused the dumb to speak.

Chapter 5

THE SOUNDS OF SILENCE

THE WORDS of Christian worship have ever acknowledged their own limit. Like all true symbols, they contain within themselves denial of their own adequacy. Before the command to be still and know God, all sounds are harsh. In response to the great pronouncement "The Lord is in his holy temple," worshipers have sought at all times to keep silence before him.

From very early days in the Church, silent prayer seems to have had a place in the context of liturgical worship. In his vision of heavenly worship, the Seer of the Apocalypse reports that between the song before the throne of God and the sound of seven trumpets, there was silence in heaven for about half an hour. Massey Shepherd, in suggesting that the structure of the Book of Revelation reflects the early Church's celebration of the Pascha, saw a parallel between this half-hour pause and the silent prayers of worshipers awaiting the newly baptized at the end of the Easter vigil.[1]

The practice known both in the East and the West whereby the priest recites the Eucharistic prayer inaudibly has been defended as a form of liturgical silence, appropriate to the awe and mystery surrounding the holy moments of consecration and communion. One ancient homily from the Eastern Church tells us that the whole ecclesiastical body observed silence between the *Sursum corda* and the *Sanctus,* while "all set themselves to pray earnestly in their hearts." [2] After "deep silence and peaceful calm settles," the preacher explains, the priest speaks to God in secret, then raises his voice at the end of his prayer so that the people may respond *Amen.*

Although this practice cannot be firmly dated before the sixth century, it has been conjectured that the custom began at least a hundred years earlier in Orthodox churches using the liturgies of St. Chrysostom and St. Basil.[3] In the West a like practice is known from at least the eighth century. The so-called "mystical" spirit behind this custom is fully audible in a well-known eucharistic hymn adapted from the Liturgy of St. James:

> Let all mortal flesh keep silence
> > And with fear and trembling stand.
> Ponder nothing earthly minded,
> > For with blessing in his hand,
> Christ our Lord to earth descendeth
> > Our full homage to demand.

Such words support Rudolf Otto's belief that silence is man's spontaneous reaction to the experience of numinous presence, to God-in-the-midst.[4] Yet silence in this full sense is not a prominent feature in liturgical worship which centers on the Word of God. Actual Christian practice is better reflected by the index of an 858-page book on liturgy and worship which has only one entry for silence—directing the reader to a nine-page "supplementary essay." [5] And it is therefore not surprising to find in the Church recurring protests against the tyranny of man-made sound.

Christian tradition knows, in fact, a constant verbal iconoclasm—the temporal counterpart of a continuing movement against all efforts to reproduce images of that which surpasses imagination. Three kinds of verbal iconoclasm seem to me to reflect the same rebellion against any idea that words are a sufficient response to the Word. One advocates silence in order that the individual may hear the voice of God; the contemplative monk is a prime example. The second calls for silence in order that God may speak to the community gathered in worship; the Society of Friends is a prime example. The third moves in an apparently opposite direction but with a like intent, testifying to the Logos who defies the logic of men's minds. Pentecostal speaking in tongues, as much as monastic retreat and Quaker meeting, appears to judge human tendencies to think that the Spirit of God can be ordered about by sound.

Best known of contemporary spokesmen for the monastic ideal is undoubtedly the Trappist monk Thomas Merton. His death in December, 1968, was reported in the same issue of *The New York Times*[6] which announced also the death of Karl Barth, best known of contemporary spokesmen for the Word of God. Through juxtaposing pictures of the two men, the *Times* curiously underlined the fact that silence is one consistent response to the Word in Christian history. The fact that Merton died in Bangkok, where he had gone to attend a religious conference, is also a reminder of the prominent role silence plays in Oriental religious thought. His last published book was appropriately on *Mystics and Zen Masters*.

While still an undergraduate at Columbia University, according to his own account in the one-time best seller, *The Seven Storey Mountain,* Thomas Merton was already active in a personal search for God. That search led him ultimately to a monastery following the rule of Cistercians of the Strict Observance. The same individual quest remains a dominant theme of his subsequent defense of monastic life in *The Waters of Siloe* and *The Silent Life.*

A cenobitic monk, living in community, Merton yet extols the solitary hermit as his ideal. The true monastic outlook, he says, is "the horizon of the desert" where the monk's ears are attuned "to the silence of the far mountains." [7] He argues that the Rule of St. Benedict is written for men who are to live "in the direct line of the pure, ancient tradition" of the Desert Fathers. He thinks community-minded interpreters of the

Benedictine Rule have too often denied or underestimated its implicit orientation toward the solitude of the hermit.[8]

Following this singular bent, Merton elaborates a theory of silence which links it closely to living alone with God. "Corporate and liturgical prayer are indeed important in the life of the Church . . . ," he admits; "but they do not of themselves satisfy the deep need for intimate contact with God in solitary prayer. . . ."[9] Although Merton ties this need to the peculiar vocation of the contemplative soul, his words speak for many Christian worshipers who hear no call to the monastery nor to full-time contemplation. They would agree with him that the eucharistic communion must be extended in "silent and solitary adoration."

The Trappist's apologia for the silent life touches two poles of general Christian experience today—the increasing clangor of our world, on the one hand, and the "mystery of divine silence" on the other. Both ideas are stressed by many who campaign for more silent time in worship. Ten years in the quietude of rural Kentucky did not drown the sounds of Broadway at 116th Street in Merton's ears. The mighty of the world, he well remembers, "accomplish their works with great noise, with speeches and drums and loud-speakers and brass and the thunder of bombers."[10] The spirit of the world makes everyman loud with the fear of his own hollowness. He cannot stop his talk about the World Series and the Rose Bowl and the weather, because silence makes him nervous.[11]

"But God works in silence," the monk believes. His Spirit teaches men not to be afraid of it, but "to find themselves in quiet."[12] The work of the Holy Spirit is integral to Merton's view of the capacity and the depths of silence. "We did not come here for the scenery, the architecture, the fresh air, the music, the country life, or for human friendship," he writes of himself and his brothers at Gethsemane; "we were brought here to be sanctified by the Holy Ghost—first, no doubt, as individuals but also together as a community."[13] The monks therefore, it is said, "lead one another to the eternal fountains of silence in which they drink the living waters and the rich wine of the Holy Spirit." [14] These are the waters Isaiah hears, waters "that flow in silence" (6:8). The biblical verse provided Merton with the title for his book and with the text for his life.

Men who would give ear to these waters, our contemplative spokesman goes on, must enter the classroom of the Holy Spirit, the *auditorium Spiritus* of which St. Bernard of Clairvaux preached. To Bernard as to Brother M. Louis (known in the world as Thomas Merton), it was clear that the Holy Spirit speaks only to the humble. To a humble soul in a state of silence and receptivity, they testify, the Holy Spirit makes known mysteries of the Kingdom of God and teaches riches of the love of Christ.

It is interesting to note that Thomas Merton's mother was a member of the Society of Friends. Except for the fact that they write more exclusively in the plural, Quaker apologists for silence sound remarkably like the monks. The Quaker experience of silent worship, "the way of wonder," is the main court of appeal for Rudolf Otto's early plea that Protestant worship should recover through silence the ancient heritage of the Spirit.[15]

Typical of the rigorously corporate concept of silence in Quaker thought is the description of the gathered meeting by the modern Friend Thomas Kelly. As author of the still-cherished *Testament of Devotion*, Kelly is widely known beyond the Society of which he was a member. Many think of him not only as an erstwhile professor at Haverford College, but more especially as a modern saint, one whose life demonstrated "the reality of the spiritual world" about which he wrote with self-authenticating assurance: "In the Quaker practice of group worship on the basis of silence come special times when an electric hush and solemnity and depth of power steal over the worshippers. A blanket of divine covering comes over the room, and a quickening Presence pervades us, breaking down some part of the special privacy and isolation of our individual lives and blending our spirits within a super-individual Life and Power. . . ." [16]

When one Friend speaks in such a silence, Kelly continues, the words connect closely to the thoughts everyone is already pursuing. "Silence becomes a bridge, not of separation but of communication." As this Quaker understands what happens to him in Meeting—although the encounter is acknowledged to be ineffable, incapable of full expression—God himself reveals himself there. A truly gathered meeting rests upon the Real Presence of God in the midst of the worshipers, he insists; and no merely psychological interpretation of the phenomenon can do justice to the group experience involved.

Freely admitting that not all silent times achieve this quality, however, Kelly is willing to identify some of the conditions which appear to promote a gathered meeting. Among them he names the need for some individuals who come to the meeting already "silently deep in active adoration." In a meeting influenced by such persons, he reports, even an unbroken silence can effect spiritual change. If words are spoken, they do not really break the silence but rather continue it, he contends, especially if the speaker uses appropriately open-ended words, restrained and allusive. Given language of this quality, "in the silences of our hearts the Holy Presence completes the unfinished words far more satisfyingly."

Whether or not a meeting achieves the conscious level of a powerfully speaking silence, Kelly alleges, it can nevertheless be considered a good meeting. Not warm feelings but offered wills really count in the "silent work of worship," as he understands it. The process of learning to accept without dismay what Kelly calls "spiritual weather" requires going deeper "in will" into God.

Such stress on active human willing as an essential ingredient in true silence comes close to the Trappist demand for discipline in a man who wants to learn contemplation. This and many other Quaker descriptions of "centering down" also use a language of depth similar to that in monastic writ-

ings. In both cases the silence being described is not a mere
cessation of noise but a positive dynamic state—the very opposite of a dead silence. It should also be noted that, for all
his stress on the community, Kelly pays tribute to the role of
individuals who come prepared. A like interdependence is assumed in Merton's thought, which holds that all of the faithful
are united in such a manner that the whole communion of
saints is present in the hermit's cell.

As Dante approaches the presence of God, toward the end
of the *Paradiso,* he is given a new guide for the rest of his
journey—St. Bernard of Clairvaux, father of the Cistercians.
Both natural reason and revealed theology give way to contemplation. At this point in the pilgrimage, human words
break down. Coming "to the eternal from the temporal, from
Florence to a people just and sane," Dante prefers to hear no
sound and to speak no words at all. He acknowledges the im-
possibility of conveying the least part of the gladness of what
he sees. He compares his own words then to infant babblings.[17]

The response of silence testifies to one limit of human discourse in worship. Another linguistic frontier has manifested
itself throughout Christian history. Those who have crossed
that frontier to speak in tongues have also been compared with
children learning to talk through using nonsense syllables. The
natural reason and the revealed theology of established
churches have been so ineffective in efforts to understand this,
that one wonders if the poet might not prove a better guide.
Just as monastic and Quaker silence are interpreted by insiders
with reference to the work of the Holy Spirit, so is that untranslatable language of *glossolalia* by those who speak it.

New Testament writings indicate that speaking in tongues
was part of worship, and already a cause of misunderstanding,
in at least some early Christian churches. At Caesarea, according to Acts, even before Peter finished preaching the
good news to Cornelius and his household, some of his listeners were "speaking in tongues and extolling God." (10:46)
At Ephesus, also according to Acts, Paul himself was the
agent of the Holy Spirit when disciples spoke with tongues

(19:6). The outbreak of tongues at Pentecost is clearly identified as an utterance given by the Holy Spirit (2:4).

The chief reference to the subject in the New Testament,
however, appears in Paul's letter to Corinth, as part of an extended discussion of spiritual gifts. Interpreters who distrust
ecstatic outbursts in worship tend to emphasize Chapter 14,
ending with Paul's judgment that in church he would rather
speak five words with his mind in order to instruct others,
"than ten thousand words in a tongue" (14:19). Interpreters
trying to defend charismatic expression tend, rather, to emphasize Chapter 12, which begins with the recognition that
the Spirit of God gives some members of the body the gift of
various kinds of tongues (12:10). Both groups sometimes
overlook the fact that the hymn on Christian love which connects the two parts of the discussion refers explicitly to the
phenomenon of glossolalia: "If I speak with the tongues of
men and of angels, but have not love, I am a noisy gong or
a clanging cymbal" (13:1).

Our interest at the moment is not in the critical problems
with which these New Testament passages abound, but rather
in the fact that modern Pentecostals appeal to all of them together as the biblical basis for their doctrine. They conclude
from them that whenever the charismatic impartation of the
Holy Spirit is described in the New Testament, "the outward
expression is an ecstatic speaking in a language that the person
had never learned." [18] The phenomenon of glossolalia is always understood as the result of a prior action by God and as
a manifestation of a continuing relationship with him.

Historians find such utterances of spiritual ecstasy breaking
forth again and again in Christian life—among the Mon-
tanists in Asia and North Africa in Tertullian's day, among
radical Anabaptist groups in sixteenth century France. They
trace antecedents of the modern recurrence to the late nineteenth century Holiness Movement in the United States, itself
an outgrowth of Methodism. But they agree that the Pentecostal Movement in its contemporary form grows out of a
Kansas college in 1901, and widens into an international

movement five years later following revival meetings in Los Angeles.

Today there are Pentecostal churches on every continent. Over twenty-five separate denominational groups are at work in the United States alone, of which the Church of God, the Assemblies of God, and the Church of God in Christ are among the largest. The common denominator among all of them is belief in baptism in the Holy Spirit of which the sign is speaking in tongues.

Early accounts of Pentecostal worship emphasize spontaneity and freedom, and the active presence of the Holy Spirit. Worship is a "charismatic happening." [19] One pioneer in the Movement describes it in these terms: "The meetings began spontaneously and as of themselves, with testimonies, prayer, thanksgiving and adoration. We never heard that somebody ought to be brief, as is often otherwise the case, because there was no definite programme that should be finished in a fixed time. The Lord's time was ours. And we had constantly new, fresh testimonies from daily experiences with God." [20]

A 1906 issue of *The Apostolic Faith*, the early publication of the Movement, reports: "Many have received the gift of singing as well as speaking in the inspiration of the Spirit. The Lord is giving new voices, he translates old songs into new tongues, he gives the music that is being sung by the angels and has a heavenly choir all singing the same heavenly song in harmony. It is a beautiful music, no instruments are needed in the meetings." [21] Still another early source testifies: "If a Mexican or a German cannot speak English he gets up and speaks in his own tongue and feels quite at home, for the Spirit interprets through his face and the people say 'Amen.' " [22] Clearly glossolalia as such is already only a part of Pentecostal worship.

As Pentecostal churches have grown and prospered, some of the early spontaneity has been lost from regular Sunday morning worship. It has been noted that speaking in tongues and other charismatic manifestations are now more likely to occur in special revival meetings or other extra gatherings.[23] On Sundays the normal service is a variation on the Service of the Word—a combination of hymns, prayers, preaching, and often (but not always) scripture reading. The old ideal of freedom remains, however. One leader maintains that if you always know what is going to happen next, a Pentecostal meeting is "back-slidden." [24]

The Pentecostal Movement is still expanding at such a rate that it increasingly commands serious attention from ecumenically minded Christians. Attempts to weigh the significance of the Movement now appear both in popular magazines and in scholarly journals. Occasionally these rise to impressive heights of critical sanity and sympathy, as in the paper read to an Ecumenical Symposium by Kilian McDonnell, O.S.B., in October, 1966.

Because glossolalia is decreasing as Pentecostalism grows, McDonnell thinks that "the question of tongues is essentially peripheral." [25] The central question posed for the established churches, as he sees it, is the question of holiness, of the manifest call to a life lived in obedience to the Spirit, and therefore in closeness to God. In a spirit approaching Pentecostal freedom, the Benedictine wonders aloud if St. Paul might not feel "more at home in the free fervor of a Pentecostal prayer meeting than in the organized dullness of our liturgical celebrations." He asks whether good order demands "that the Spirit submit his inspirations in advance for an imprimatur?" [26]

Few outside observers manage such openness and candor, however. For the most part the field is still dominated by psychological and sociological interpretations of Pentecostalism which seek to write the Movement off with variations on the themes of neurotic emotional outlet or "religion of the Oppressed" respectively. In sharp contrast are the estimates made by Pentecostals themselves, who voice joyous eschatological expectations. As one speaker at the 1955 World Pentecostal

Conference in Stockholm put it: "I believe that we ourselves, the Pentecostal revival, represent . . . a token that Jesus' coming is at hand." [27]

From what we have said so far it would appear that Pentecostal worship might well be considered a kind of liturgical iconoclasm, protesting against fixed forms in worship, but not necessarily against language intended to communicate from man to man. As our earlier commentator observed, there is time in Pentecostal worship to listen to everyone. They are operating on "the Lord's time," not a tight Sunday morning schedule. We have yet to consider, however, that phenomenon now known as Neo-Pentecostalism, that outbreak of charismatic fervor in their midst which so scandalized some churchmen a decade ago.

When, in the late fifties and early sixties, speaking in tongues began manifesting itself in conservative congregations from coast to coast, some of the press and some of the church leaders rushed to psychotherapists for interpretations. They were given a full bag of theories including hysteria, latent psychosis, exhibitionism, mass hypnosis, and an outpouring of the collective unconscious understood in Jungian terms. Others turned to linguists for analysis of tape recordings, and were rewarded with the information that the sounds were non-words, not part of any known human language, although they came closest to some of the Malayo-Polynesian dialects. Those who experienced glossolalia believed they were praising the Lord.

One Lutheran pastor explained that in order to speak in tongues "you have to quit praying in English." Gradually as "the lips and tongue begin to move more freely," he maintained, "the Spirit will begin to shape a beautiful language of prayer and praise." [28] A Baptist minister reported his unexpected experience in these words: "I began to praise the Lord, and in this spirit of praise I began to say words I did not know." [29] An Episcopalian testified that he "felt and heard the winds" as if every window in the place were suddenly opened. [30]

Apparently during this period of great public interest in charismatic phenomena, tongues were heard most frequently in small groups, often meeting in homes or in college dormitories; but Saturday night prayer services in at least one Presbyterian church are said regularly to have drawn several hundred people. A popular magazine account of one of these meetings in exurban Philadelphia emphasizes its fast-moving pace and the high degree of direct participation by laymen. Of considerable interest is the reporter's description of what happened when the minister asked the congregation just to praise the Lord: "Some of the people began singing in low chanting tones that rose and fell in a sort of liturgical pattern. . . . The singing ended very suddenly, as if by signal, though there *was* no signal, and the hall became profoundly silent. Into the silence a woman began to speak in tongues. Her voice was tiny, and, but for the depth of the silence, would have been lost. . . ." [31] It would seem that in this case silence had again made it possible for people to speak and to hear in new ways.

Thoughtful persons who considered without panic this resurgence of charismatic speaking found in it both a commentary on conformist society and a commentary on the freedom of God the Holy Spirit. Glossolalia was linked with other volcanic forces erupting in our culture which people find equally difficult to face. It was dubbed "LSD evangelism," offering a soul-shaking experience comparable to that sought by the drug-users. It was suggested that the movement is evidence of rebellion against materialistic worldviews, and a demand for emotional honesty, an affirmation of authentic selfhood in depersonalized society. It was also suggested that what was happening in the churches through glossolalia parallels what has been happening in the arts, especially through abstract expressionism. Perhaps in both cases, underground man is being prepared for an underground god? [32]

Those who would ponder the meaning of ecstatic speech into silence do well to pursue the idea that it is related to what is happening in the arts today. In drama, in music, in literature and its criticism, as well as in the visual arts, a move toward silence is apparent. Beckett's *Act Without Words,* John Cage's *Silence,* Susan Sontag's *Against Interpretation* are all outward and visible symptoms of a general cultural trend—a trend which George Steiner has characterized as "The Retreat from the Word."

As a composer, John Cage is, of course, not retreating from words when he retreats into silence. Nor is silence the opposite of sound. There is no such thing as silence, as Cage understands it. He returns again and again in his writing to his own 1951 discovery in an anechoic chamber, a laboratory for scientific experiment as soundproof as was then technologically possible. To his unending surprise, he heard his own nervous system and his own blood circulating.

"Something is always happening that makes a sound," Cage says.[33] He is interested in all the time arts—dance, music, poetry—all of which are not saying something but doing something, he insists. "Time," he says, "(so many minutes so many seconds) is what we and sounds happen in."[34] What we call silence is simply duration, time for hearing otherwise unheeded sound.

Both the positive and the negative aspects of his aesthetic of silence speak to the kind of verbal iconoclasm we have said to be perennial in Christian worship. The negative dimension of his thinking reflects, in part, his fascination with Zen. It betrays an anti-intellectual stance, comparable to that expressed by some Neo-Pentecostals. Listening is best, he says, in a state of mental emptiness.[35] All old sounds appear to be worn out by intellectualization, as he put it in a 1959 lecture; but in silence, through silence, one can begin to hear the old sounds he had thought worn out by thinking—quiet sounds like love and friendship. "If one stops thinking about them, suddenly they are fresh and new."[36]

All music is composed of sounds and silences, of course. By using more silence, this composer intends to stop imposing his will on others. He deliberately strips his mind of its right to control. Freed from predetermined limits to the universe of possibilities, the minds of his listeners are freed for the act of listening. Neither composer nor listener, Cage suggests, is able to improve on creation.

To read John Cage is to be reminded of Jesus' saying, "do not be anxious how or what you are to answer or what you are to say, for the Holy Spirit will teach you in that very hour what you ought to say" (Luke 12:12). This saying has often been used in defense of extempore prayer in Christian worship. Applied to silence in Cage's terms, it becomes a deliberate checking of habits of speaking and hearing for the sake of greater freshness and of more faithful reception of experience. Positively, he understands silence as an opening of doors to what is happening in the environment. "We need not fear these silences, we may love them," he says with a change of metaphor; "it is like an empty glass into which at any moment anything may be poured." [37]

That "anything" is precisely what troubles many critics of ecstatic worship in all its forms. One must discern the spirits, as St. Paul well knew. The demonic can ride into silence along with or instead of the Holy Spirit. The great voice, as it seems to me, of George Steiner has reckoned more adequately with this dual possibility of silence, in worship as in literature.

In several of the essays collected in *Language and Silence,* as well as in the one called "The Retreat from the Word," Steiner probes the revaluation of silence which he finds to be characteristic of the modern spirit. Two of the reasons he discerns for the new attempts to transcend language in the Western world deeply affect worshipers as well as the artists of whom he is speaking.

First, the language of mathematics is growing progressively untranslatable, Steiner notes, while larger and larger areas of human life are being submitted to its modes and proceedings. "Those of us who are compelled by our ignorance of exact science to imagine the universe through a veil of non-mathematical language inhabit an animate fiction. The actual facts of the case—the space-time continuum of relativity, the atomic structure of all matter, the wave-particle state of energy—are no longer accessible through the word. It is no paradox to assert that in cardinal respects reality now begins *outside* verbal language." [38] Many have accepted intellectually such a shrinkage in the reality to which words give access, but "except in moments of bleak clarity" few have allowed it to change their ways of thinking and acting and communicating.

Secondly, and perhaps even more seriously, language has been poisoned, Steiner believes, by political inhumanity in our time. He writes eloquently of the injury done to language in Nazi Germany—of German writers who "despaired of their instrument" and wrote no more "because their language had served at Belsen, because words could be found for all those things and men were not struck dumb for using them." [39]

But the widespread sense of a death in language which he observes goes far beyond the terrible possibility of "no poetry after Auschwitz." Mass culture as a whole brutalizes language. By citing and documenting Ionesco's journal entry "a civilization of words is a civilization distraught," [40] Steiner forces one to listen with new ears to the surfeit of tarnished words heard selling diet cola and antiballistic missiles and presidential candidates. Perhaps in growing so wasteful of words, he suggests in another essay, our culture has "cheapened or spent what assurance of perception and numinous value they once contained." [41]

Steiner himself cannot admit this, however. He is a man dedicated to words. Just at the point when his reader is persuaded that words are too tainted to use in speaking to reality, he reminds him of the ambiguity of silence, too. It can function as a wall as well as a window. It can open onto darkness as well as onto light.

In a 1966 essay called "Postscripts," [42] Steiner hears as "the memory of hope" the last message to reach the outside world from the Warsaw ghetto in 1940: "In the Warsaw ghetto a child wrote in its diary: 'I am hungry, I am cold; when I grow up I want to be a German, and then I shall no longer be hungry, and no longer cold.' And now I want to write that sentence again: 'I am hungry, I am cold; when I grow up I want to be a German, and then I shall no longer be hungry, and no longer cold.' And say it many times over, in prayer for the child, in prayer for myself. Because when that sentence was written I was fed, beyond my need, and slept warm, and was silent." [43]

Perhaps men are beginning to hear this loud silence today. Some who do equate all silence, therefore, with indifference. They claim that silence and indifference together poison every aspect of our human existence. They institute nonstop talk-ins "to teach the silent to speak out, and the deaf to listen." [44] Following John Cage, Marshall McLuhan defines silence as "the unheeded world." [45] The lyrics of the song from which our chapter title was taken put forth the same idea in their own version of speaking in tongues. Simon and Garfunkel convince and convict when they see prophetic words scrawled on the walls of tenements—and when they hear them whispered in the sounds of silence.

Worshipers straining toward silence today, whether through non-words or no words, are straining toward that time when all men shall respond to the words of the Prophets. A new hope for such a time has manifested itself in current thought to such a degree that this hope must be the focus of our next chapter.

Chapter 6

WORSHIP AND HOPE

SO FAR in description of Christian worship, we have said that the early Christians eagerly looked forward in their meetings to the return of Christ. We have emphasized the fact that they developed their own rhythm of time, in enjoyment and in expectation of the Eighth Day. We have noted that they still proclaim and summon a future Kingdom in sounds, and await it in silences. And we have acknowledged—although perhaps not sufficiently—that this eschatological stress is characteristic of very contemporary writing about liturgy. When one reads worship studies written before 1950, the eschatological bell does not ring so loudly.[1]

In the same twenty years, and most especially in the last five, the Christian Church has suddenly been made conscious of a new theology of hope. A measle-like outbreak of interest in the idea recently reached almost epidemic proportions. *New Theology No. 5,* published in 1968, and the symposium on HOPE, to which the summer issue of the journal *Cross Currents* was devoted in the same year, well illustrate the wide range of writing on the subject.[2] A national theological colloquium addressed itself to similar questions in its 1968 assembly; a sectional meeting of the American Academy of Religion made hope its topic in 1969.

This intellectual phenomenon shows curious interconnections with contemporary understanding of worship which deserve our attention. How Christians think about God necessarily influences the ways they act out their cultic response to him; the forms of their worship influence in turn the doctrines they develop and defend. Such a two-way street between theology and worship is widely recognized; but the heavy traffic on it deserves more study. At least one observer has attributed the theological revival of eschatology directly to the liturgical movement.[3]

It is pointless to defend such a chicken-and-egg argument. Whatever the merits of claiming logical priority for man's experience of God in worship, an experience which he later elaborates in terms of its intellectual implications, no historical community of faith now offers this pure option. Thought and worship have been going on together in the Church from very early on the morning of the first Easter. Both activities have influenced each other through two millennia.

The idea of an ecology of faith recognizes this organic situation. Pioneer naturalist John Muir summed it up beautifully, in fact, when he said (in another connection) that as soon as he tried to pick out anything by itself, he found it hitched to everything in the universe. The question of how liturgy and theology are interrelated is nevertheless forced upon us by our description of the temporal and dynamic phenomena in worship. Have we been unduly influenced by the theological mood of the day?

In part, no doubt, the new theological talk is yet another reflection of our general cultural crisis. The future tense, as George Steiner noted in a review of *The Biological Time Bomb*,[4] is always a scandal. Current events conspire to make it also a terror. "I think the signs are all pointing the wrong way," C. P. Snow said not long ago; "the objective grounds for hope have gotten less and the objective grounds for non-hope have gotten stronger."[5] A Nobel prize physicist has asked: "What is left to hope for?"[6] As the "Generation in Search of a Future"[7] appears to know very well indeed, man's chance to go on is in question.

Responding to this mood of profound hopelessness,

prophets of hope have arisen—indeed a whole school of hope, with Marxist, Humanist, and Christian members of the faculty. By rescuing Marxist eschatology from determinist interpretations, Ernst Bloch unquestionably did much to stimulate present rethinking of the concept. By listening to Bloch, theologians like Harvey Cox have found ways out of the God-is-dead *cul de sac*.[8] We will listen, however, to three other current and hopeful voices—those of Erich Fromm in his remarkable manifesto, *The Revolution of Hope*; of Jürgen Moltmann in *Theology of Hope*; and of Dietrich Ritschl in his *Memory and Hope*. All three writers say something directly about worship, but in different tones.

I have chosen these three because they illustrate three possible approaches to the relationship between thought and worship. Moltmann stresses the priority of theology. Christian belief leads to certain kinds of worship and is opposed to other kinds. Ritschl stresses the priority of worship. Christian experience in worship leads to certain kinds of theology and stands in judgment on others. Only the humanist appears to me to show adequate awareness of the full mutuality between, to use useful shorthand, creed and cult.

Fromm's urgent call for a revolt against depersonalizing technology was hurried through the press. It shows signs of being hastily written, and it draws heavily on his own earlier works. Yet it is significantly freer than most of them in its use of religious language, and more revealing of the roots which support this attractive form of secular humanism.

Our current social plight arises, Fromm says, frcm idolatry. Man has bowed down to the machines he has made. God can no longer bring certainty, but the computer can: "Our age has found a substitute for God: the impersonal calculation. This new god has turned into an idol to whom all men may be sacrificed. A new concept of the sacred and unquestionable is arising: that of calculability, probability, factuality."[9] Considered psychologically, the sacrificial victims exhibit several pathological symptoms. One is passiveness. Having turned ourselves into bored consumers, we are essentially dead men.

The "well-adjusted" members of the herd counterfeit hope, Fromm observes, through a kind of resigned optimism; but this is really just the non-hope of Kafka's man waiting outside the open door of heaven. Others respond to their loss of hope with "hardening of the heart"; they freeze emotionally and isolate themselves from their fellow men. This response is another pathological symptom in the total syndrome of alienation which he is diagnosing. The "new man of the technectronic age" is, in fact, beginning to suffer from a "low-grade chronic schizophrenia." [10] Because he has split his emotions from his thinking, the former deteriorate into neurotic passions and the latter into machine-like intellectual activity.

Hope, which is essential to a healthy society and to healthy personal life, Fromm argues, must be resurrected. He wants to use that word "without any reference to its theological implications in Christianity," although he admits that the Christian meaning would be "one of the possible symbolic expressions." [11] Prophetic messianic hope, offering real freedom to decide in the present, must be recaptured. This hope, he thinks, was kept alive in the concept of the "Second Coming," in spite of an apocalyptic shift toward determinism, and in spite of the fact that "the Church usually retreated to a position of passive waiting." [12]

Such a resurrection of hope will be possible, Fromm continues, if we actively develop a counter-revolution toward humane experiences, if we consciously seek to develop "frames of orientation and devotion." Underlying his catalogue of humane experiences is the concept of transcendence, a concept he interprets nontheistically: "If we speak of transcendence in a non-theological sense, there is no need for the concept of God. However, the psychological reality is the same. The basis for love, tenderness, compassion, interest, responsibility, and identity is precisely that of being versus having, *and that means* transcending the ego. It means letting go of one's greed, making oneself empty in order to fill oneself, making oneself poor in order to be rich." [13]

To achieve such transcendence, man must become *homo*

ludens: "Activeness on the trans-survival level is what one calls play," Fromm writes, "or all those activities related to cult, ritual, and art." [14] Although historically religion was almost the only system which incorporated these aspects of human experience, he thinks we must now promote active participant culture in other ways. His program of social planning calls for encouraging such arts as dancing, music, reading, and little theatre groups. It also calls for developing, within all social institutions, participant face-to-face groups for information exchange, debate, and decision-making.

Psychospiritual renewal will result from such a program, Fromm believes. And this psychospiritual renewal will in turn produce common rituals and symbols "because these will grow naturally once the soil is prepared." [15] The humanist rituals he foresees include both songs and group silence. His suggested symbols are the dove and the other currently popular symbol of peace: ☮

From the perspective of a Jürgen Moltmann trying to recover eschatology from the appendix of the theological textbook, such a humanist manifesto would be merely evidence of the utopian spirit which he thinks always manifests itself in time of crisis. Not surprisingly, one critical review of Moltmann's *Theology of Hope* asks where the book makes contact with post-Christian secular ideology.[16] In spite of his efforts to be responsive to the "modern consciousness," and in spite of his efforts to correct the thought of Karl Barth at many points, Moltmann is writing theology in the classic style of that master. He believes that Christian eschatology must be sharply distinguished from utopian thought, because it speaks of Jesus Christ and his future. Easter makes hope for Christ's future possible. The "hopeful theological mind" is at work to span the future horizon projected by the Easter event.[17]

When he comes at the end of his book to apply his eschatological thought to Christians in modern society, Moltmann admits that the Church has lost its character of *cultus publicus.* He argues that it must resist the alternative roles society would like to assign to it as a religion. If it is true to the New

Testament, the Church cannot allow itself to be a socially irrelevant *cultus privatus,* nor a cult of a new subjectivity, nor "a kind of Noah's ark for men in their social estrangement." [18] Rather it must be the exodus church, going forth into the world to turn expectation into present activity for creative reshaping of society.

Worship therefore serves to provide men with a meaningful horizon of expectation. Christians gather as a waiting, expectant congregation, seeking communion with the Coming Lord. He gives them power and freedom to expose themselves to the pain of the negative, as they expend themselves in work for the world. Moltmann interprets three elements of worship —Word, Baptism, and the Lord's Supper—all as oriented toward the future; but his Reformation emphasis is on the first. The prime function of the cult is to pro-claim and to pro-ject the horizon of the expectation of the Kingdom of God.

Moltmann reaches this consistently eschatological idea of the pilgrim people of God only after a thorough examination of both Old and New Testament thought, as well as of more recent philosophies of history. In light of the criticism of Mircea Eliade which we proposed in Chapter 1, when describing a *Marana tha* dimension of worship, it is especially pertinent to note the use Moltmann makes of Eliade's thought in these central chapters.

When the old nomad religion of the Hebrews, with its "vectoral and kinaesthetic elements," met the static religion of the Canaanite peasants, Moltmann argues, it did not abandon the God of promise. He rejects Eliade's idea that the cultus always seeks hierophanies at sacred places and at sacred times. Israel was "but little concerned to understand the meaning of the 'appearances' of Yahweh in terms of such hallowing of places and times." [19] Contrary to worshiping in a mythical world, as Eliade suggests, Israel's cultic interest was in uttering the word of divine promise. Accordingly she not only historicized, but also futurized Canaanite festivals. Eschatological thinking is opposed to mythological thinking in Moltmann's view. He interprets both prophetic thought and its apocalyptic derivative as directed toward an eschaton "wider" than the beginning ever was.

In the ensuing chapter on New Testament eschatology, Greek epiphany religions take the place of Canaanite religion as the villain of the story of syncretism. Paul's quarrel with the Corinthians, as Moltmann reads the evidence, is clearly over eschatology. Paul insists on a future eschatology of the cross which is "hostile to every eschatological ecstasy of fulfillment." [20] All Hellenistic forms of sacramental thinking are criticized for reducing eschatology to a point where it remains only subliminally, if at all.

Eliade enters once again in the next chapter as a representative spokesman for an ancient Greek way of thinking about tradition which is opposed both to Israel's idea of promise and to the Christian idea of proclaiming the gospel. The antithetical Christian concept of tradition allows it to see the future in the past, Moltmann insists, and thus to move forward in mission to all people: "The Christian mission has no cause to enter into an alliance with romanticist nihilism against the revolutionary progressiveness of the modern age and to present its own tradition as a haven of traditionalism for a contemporary world now grown uncertain and weary of hoping." [21] In this markedly Protestant manner, Moltmann has sought to put a future orientation back into Christian thought and worship, in order both to be faithful to the biblical emphasis on the coming Lord, and to provide a new dynamic openness to service in the world.

Working independently, another theologian of hope, Dietrich Ritschl, reached many of the same conclusions but by a radically different route. His Christological study, *Memory and Hope,* was published in 1967, the same year that the English translation of Moltmann's work appeared.[22] For Ritschl, the impasse of theology can be broken and an active hope arise to give Christians new "access to the present," only if Western Christians learn again from the Eastern Church, and most particularly from the doxological language of Orthodox eucharistic worship.

Ritschl's key concern is with *Christus praesens,* Christ present here and now, received in the memory and the hope of the Church. He views his work as a new search for the correlation of prayer and thinking which Western theologians have too long separated. The ongoing worship of the Church has acknowledged that Jesus Christ "makes himself present," but theology has failed to deal adequately with what this means. So that God's activity in Jesus be not limited to the past, Ritschl says, the reception and interpretation of scripture and tradition must occur in the light of the *Christus praesens:* "God's ever new activity and presence in the risen Christ is to be seen as part of his ongoing faithfulness to his people. Thus the Church, when reading texts of the past, is hoping into the future, and when hoping into the future, the Church is remembering the promises of the past." [23]

Ritschl calls this "seemingly trivial" phenomenological observation of critical importance. Only when a thinking person is captured by "the faithfulness of God, expressed in the form of statement, sermons, recited creeds, hymns, deeds and promises," he declares, does he have access not only to those phenomena whose authority and validity he feels compelled to test, but also to "the peculiar logic" of God's dealing with mankind.[24]

Properly to receive these traditional texts today, therefore, one must recognize the principle of the *Christus praesens* in worship.[25] The general Western misunderstanding of patristic eschatology is the result, Ritschl argues, of our failure to realize how completely the liturgy influenced the thinking of the early Greek Fathers. They were not operating as independent philosophers, outside the framework of worship.[26] He blames Augustine for the rationalist fall which left Western theologians with a "resting and retired" God, and therefore with a static understanding of the Church and the *eschaton.* One-sided emphasis on Augustinian theology, he thinks, is responsible for the fact that eschatology finally degenerated into individualistic concern for one's own fate after death.

In contrast, when Irenaeus and Athanasius speak of last things, Ritschl observes, they do not separate their thought from the context of worship. He praises Irenaeus for unfolding "a truly eschatological idea of the incarnation," one which made it clear that the final consummation is still to be expected. It was Ritschl's special study of Athanasius, however, which led him to a new appreciation of a language with power to "explode into directness."

Doxological language is defined as "the whole complex of utterances," both in the Bible and in later Christian tradition, which are directly or indirectly related to prayer and liturgy.[27] This language is in "strange reciprocity" with theological language. The Church speaks doxological language in addressing the *Christus praesens*. Theologians must speak a different language, not the language of prayer. Nevertheless they stand in the stream of that language and must take account of it.

By his own involvement in this language, Ritschl is able to elaborate a theory of the Church's hope which begins with Easter. The earliest Christians understood this day in the categories of a new memory and a new hope, whereby Jesus had become for them the fulfillment of Israel's hope and also a new promise. In this dialectic of interchangeable terms, the author moves to the *Christus praesens* now met in worship, and there recognized as one remembered and hoped for in the future. He leads on from hope to hope to the ultimate hope—God's final fulfillment of his promises.

It is precisely this eschatological structure of faith, as Ritschl sees it, which enables the Christian to act now. "The stronger the hope, the more direct and passionate is his involvement in the present problems and tasks of the Church and the human situation generally." [28]

Their thought about hope has thus led all three representatives of the current school of prophets to acknowledge intimate connections between hope and worship. Hope, in Fromm's thought, is nourished in the human dynamics of cultural and cultic activity; hopeful people both discover and express their creative freedom in ritual and symbol. Hope in Christ, in Moltmann's thought, is nourished especially by the expectation of the Kingdom of God, proclaimed in the worshiping community and projected in service to the world. As he sees it, however, Greek thought and Hellenistic worship seriously threaten the forward and hopeful thrust of biblical faith. Emphasis on the *Christus praesens* in worship, in Ritschl's opinion, keeps theology from becoming static, rationalistic and individualistic. He finds eschatological dynamism in the very areas of Greek thought and worship which Moltmann implicitly condemned.

Even from this brief sample of the new theology of hope, I think we can draw two conclusions. First, it is evident that by attending to the experience of worship and its language, Ritschl has achieved a more balanced and more useful idea of Christian hope, because he has dealt more adequately with the past and its role in helping to determine the future. As Shunji F. Nishi has pointed out: "By restoring to history the dimension of the past, Ritschl demonstrates that a theology of hope can stand only as there is a simultaneous theology of memory." [29]

But secondly, it is therefore evident, as Moltmann also recognized, that a large part of the Christian worship tradition does not readily adapt itself to translation into terms of the future. Without sharing his devaluation of sacramental thought, one can yet agree with him that theological exposition of the Lord's Supper has not characteristically emphasized the kind of futurist eschatology he is developing. More often emphasis has been on a "realized eschatology," on a manifestation in this age of the New Age begun in Christ. As a leading liturgical scholar of the Orthodox Church expresses it, the Sacrament is, by its nature, "a victory over time and a departure out of it. . . ." [30]

Such a statement suggests that our description of worship in terms of time and its correlates is only one side of the story. Christian worship is not only a summoning of the future; it is an enactment of hope in the present. To talk of the *Christus praesens* in the liturgy, one must use images of space, sight, and bodily incarnation. Thus both theologians of hope lead us on to explore those phenomena of Christian worship which can best be understood as a shaping of the present.

PART II

Shaping the Present

Chapter 7

IN ALL PLACES

WHEN, at the beginning of the celebration of the Lord's Supper, Christians say that it is right to give thanks to God "always and everywhere"—or, in an alternative form of words, "at all times and in all places"—they affirm the spatial character of their lives. The affirmation comes at a point in the liturgical action, furthermore, immediately after representatives of the people have brought forward tangible things, bread and wine and other gifts. They are about to set a table and share a meal. Normally they are gathered together for this celebration in a building they call a church. Such activity in such a place cannot be understood only in the language of time.

Nevertheless, a deep mistrust of spatial categories in religious thinking gnaws at some Christians today. One form of the suspicion is manifest in the polarized contrast between dynamic and static worship, which we have already noted more than once. Another form calls for a wholesale rejection in the Space Age of bankrupt ancient metaphors. What sense does it make to "lift up our hearts" when we know that God is not up there? Modern man, it has been argued, can no longer conceive of transcendence in the idiom of space; he must be freed from bondage to topography.

Theologians who would so quickly abandon space underestimate, it seems to me, the powerful role it plays in the contemporary imagination—in the sciences as well as in the arts. One might point, for example, to Robert Ardrey's *The Territorial Imperative*; or to a report on "the most important discovery in physics of the decade" entitled *An Asymmetry in Space*. The final sentence of the article: "God is not, somehow, completely ambidextrous." [1] Or again, to director Peter Brook's lectures on the theatre of today, published as *The Empty Space*; or to Nadine Gordimer's novel *The Late Bourgeois World*, in which the protagonist, waking in the night, reflects on the "space walk" reported in the day's headlines: "What's going on overhead is perhaps the spiritual expression of our age, and we don't recognize it. Space exploration isn't a 'programme'—it's the new religion. Out of the capsule, up there, out of this world. . . . Could any act of worship as we've known such things for two thousand years express more urgently a yearning for life beyond life—the yearning for God?" [2]

Even such random evidence is enough, I believe, to show that modern man still encounters his spatial environment with a dimension of wonder. The question would appear to be not whether we are going to think about ultimate questions in terms of space, but how. For man's *Weltanschauungen,* as the Teutonic jargon would put it, are indeed rooted in his *Lebenswelt*. Something of what this means for contemporary worshipers will become apparent as we look at three phenomena related to the height and depth and breadth of Christian experience in worship. In each case the Christian landscape and the Christian mindscape appear as Siamese twins. For worshipers who take seriously the belief that the Word was made flesh and dwelt among men, this will be no surprise.

On first sight, the first phenomenon is supremely simple: The Emperor Constantine allowed Christians to build churches. Church buildings are such an accepted part of Christian institutional life today, that it is difficult to remember that for more than three hundred years they were the exception not the rule. Until the fourth century, the normal place of worship was, in effect, someone's living room, or perhaps a room on the third floor of a tenement house in Troas or

Athens.[3] Along with declaring "the peace of the Church," the Emperor not only removed restrictions on the Christian public presence, but positively encouraged a program of church construction. It has been flourishing ever since.

Real estate was not, and is not, an unmixed blessing in Christian life. In his erudite *Introduction to Liturgical Theology,* Alexander Schmemann charges that the fourth century building program contributed greatly to a radical shift in the most fundamental ideas of what the Church and its worship were all about. On the one hand, when Christians began to build basilicas modeled after Roman public buildings, Schmemann has shown, they began to conduct public ceremonies in them influenced by the ways of the imperial court. On the other hand, they developed at the same time a new interest in the places associated with heroes of the community. They came to attach special holiness to the tombs of their martyrs, and to "relics" of those giants who had died for the faith.

The reverse experience of twentieth century Russian Orthodox émigrés confirms for Schmemann the close connection between buildings and what occurs in them. When political revolution forced them out of churches to worship in garages and cellars, they discovered that pomp was out of place. Only much simpler ceremonial was appropriate to the stark surroundings. And this, he says, led them to experience more fully the essential dynamics of the liturgical act.

In Professor Schmemann's eyes, fervent interest in sacred space was a chief cause as well as a chief symptom of a new piety which emerged in the Byzantine church between the time of Constantine and the ninth century. In the process all aspects of worship gradually came to be colored by a kind of mysteriological piety, until the early church's theology of worship was transformed. It was no longer conceived as anticipation of the Kingdom of God, but rather as "a series of 'breakthroughs' into a sort of other world, as communion in a reality in no way connected with 'this world.'" [4]

The same idea still dominates Orthodoxy, Schmemann acknowledges. The liturgy is "experienced as a departure out of the world for a little while, as a 'vent' or break in earthly existence opened up for the inlet of grace." [5] Although he deplores the gradual extinction of earlier eschatological ideas of the Church and its worship, he and other Orthodox writers still use the spatial language of the Byzantine synthesis even when they are arguing for a recovery of eschatological urgency.

Because a "celestial dimension" permeates the Orthodox liturgy, one writer puts it in typical fashion, it is the task of the Church to permeate "earth with heaven." [6] Or again, another writes: "Eucharistic space is holy space. Heaven, that realm beyond space, becomes physically present in the place where the eucharist is being celebrated. It is 'Holy Land,' even as the land which the Lord blessed with His footprints is Holy Land. 'Heaven and earth are full of Thy Glory'; that happens in eucharistic space where heaven and earth meet." [7]

The author, Paul Verghese of the Syrian Orthodox Church, is well aware of the irrational sound of such language to men who suppose it is meant to be comprehended by rational analysis. He believes that worship is a "regular excursus into a nonrational expression." [8] He uses the doctrine of the Incarnation to explain why Christian worship has to draw in all elements of life and culture. Time and space categories may both be used to address the transcendent God precisely because he does not occupy either time or space. "He is not to be captured in our neat time-space categories. . . . Our Father in 'heaven' is not an object of astronomic research or space-probing. . . . He cannot be thought. He can only be worshipped. . . ." [9] And modern man, as Verghese understands him, is not able to become fully human until he learns to worship, rather than speculate about, the transcendent God.

The idea of Heaven probably ranks second only to the idea of the Second Coming of Christ in secular catalogues of the Absurd. Christians reject the literalist notion that heaven is a "where" as they know other "where's"; just as they reject the naive assumption that the Return of Christ will occur when the Great Earthquake comes. Atomic physicist-priest William Pollard has suggested that modern Christians must invent a new spatial imagery, to conceive of the whole space-time continuum as being "immersed in a space of higher dimensions." [10] For a scientific or mathematical mind it becomes possible to think of a kind of fifth dimensional heaven, not as above us but as perpendicular to ordinary space.

The Syrian Orthodox theologian has been saying that we must at one and the same time reject all efforts to dwarf God into our man-sized mental models, and nevertheless accept the spatial as well as the temporal metaphors with which he may be addressed in worship. For we have, after all, no other language. All language is conditioned by our space-formed lives. His appeal to the doctrine of the Incarnation includes an appeal to the space-informed selfhood of Jesus from Nazareth in Galilee, whom Christians believe meets them in the breaking of the bread.

The very fact of buildings called churches, quite apart from the shape of them, apparently encouraged natural human tendencies among Christians to relate the object of worship to the space in which he was worshiped, and to adapt their thinking accordingly. Although they know that God is not subject to a "where," Christians continue to speak in worship of his "where" as heaven. That such language is by no means limited to Eastern Orthodox writers is well illustrated by the contemporary Protestant statement that God's presence in worship means "an irruption here below of the world to come: heaven on earth." [11]

Orientation, a second phenomenon illustrating the complexity of spatial experience in Christian worship, also grows directly out of Constantine's building program. In the liturgical movement today there is much emphasis on the Holy Communion being celebrated with the minister facing the people across the table, in the manner of the early church and in the manner most expressive of a theology of the people of God. This position is known technically as the "Westward" position, in contradistinction to the "Eastward" position, whereby a priest celebrates facing the altar and with his back to the people.

These directional signals arose, of course, from the custom of building churches "oriented" toward the East. Because of it, the facade of a church building came to be spoken of as the west end, even if it faced south-south-east. The altar end was necessarily the east end.

One liturgical scholar interprets this convention as the inevitable consequence of building basilicas in the Roman style. They were long narrow buildings, so that the natural focus was toward the end. The borrowed shape necessarily gave a "directional bias" to worship. This directional bias, he believes, developed ideas of orientation, by which the east was understood either to symbolize the rising sun and hence Christ as the Light of the World, or alternatively to symbolize Jerusalem-Paradise, the place of the beginning and end of all things.[12]

The possibility that Christians everywhere interpreted their eastern orientation as directed toward Jerusalem is ruled out by evidence from early churches in Eastern Syria. Although they were already "east of Eden," in the terms of the symbol already alluded to, they were also carefully oriented toward the geographic east. This must reflect, according to one interpreter, an eschatological expectation of the Parousia, the idea that the Risen Christ would appear "as the last sunrise on the day of eternity." [13]

In any case, "the mentality of orientation also took the imagination outside the building," as both historians would agree.[14] East-end altars and the backs of priests produced a horizontal symbolism, and led worshipers to picture God as "out-there," beyond the east wall. By extension, orientation emphasized God's transcendence over his immanence, an emphasis continued in Gothic architecture, wherein the vista down the nave to the altar still leads man's imagination "out-there" to the majestic otherness of God.

Another liturgiologist prefers to link orientation frankly and flatly with the retention of pagan practices in Christian worship. Christians both adopted the custom of facing East for their prayers, it is explained, and of building their churches on that directional axis, because such orientation was "an old tradition among the people of Mediterranean countries and was much used in sun-worship." [15] Such an account ignores or discredits evidence that the worship of Yahweh in the temple at Jerusalem had already been given precisely the same geographic orientation, as is clear in the imagery of Ezekiel, when he beholds in his vision the glory of the God of Israel coming from the East and entering the temple by the east gate.

Orientation seems to be a basic ingredient in worship. To repudiate this symbolism just because other men in other places have thereby demonstrated that worship is one of the ways men "get their bearings," is to fall victim to what Edwyn Bevan called "anthropological intimidation." It is not necessary to label it "mythological consciousness." Ernst Cassirer has argued that the problem of orientation always starts from the experienced opposition of night and day. All zones of space therefore come to be connected with the dark-light contrast. The East is inevitably viewed as the source of light and life; the West, of death.

The politics of the Western world discourage seeing this particular significance in the points of the compass today, and so does the phenomenological view of space-perception. Merleau-Ponty, for example, demonstrates that direction is not an absolute. The results of diabolic-sounding experiments on subjects living in rooms with distorting mirrors which make everything appear at a 45-degree angle, or wearing spectacles which invert the whole world, support his argument that the body itself depends on the visual field for a sense of direction. What is right side up or upside down depends on how you look at things. But clear perception and assured action, he concluded, are possible only in a phenomenal space which is oriented.[16]

Orientation in this sense is a thoroughly faded metaphor, as it is when a Christian writer concludes his studies in sign, symbol, and meaning by defining religion as "life-orientation." But the word serves to remind us that the direction of one's gaze in worship is no more inconsequential today than it was thought to be in a Roman basilica or in Chartres Cathedral.

The third phenomenon illustrating problems of space in Christian worship can be stated quite simply. The Christian Church spread from Greenland's icy mountains to India's coral strand. One common act of worship, originated in Palestine, is now celebrated regularly in virtually every country of the world.

The ecumenical Church, in the root sense of the Church in the whole inhabited world, believes that this act is appropriate in every culture. Such a belief inevitably raises questions of variety and uniformity. How much can a single form of worship be adapted to different cultural settings without losing its essential meaning? How much uniformity of worship is necessary to keep Christians aware of their common membership in One Body?

Recent liturgical revisions have made Catholic churches newly conscious of these questions. If people are to become fully active in worship, the forms of expression must truly be theirs, not some exotic import. But developing truly indigenous liturgies may lead to radical changes in the understanding of what is being done, as well as make it more difficult to express the universality of the Church through common worship.

Use of the local language is just one piece in a larger puzzle of translation. Vatican II was fully conscious of the other issues. Commentators have noted with interest that the Constitution on the Liturgy no longer argues for retaining Latin on the grounds that it is a sign of unity, as earlier encyclicals had. Rather it assumes some use of the vernacular and in principle allows for its extension. It also encourages the use of elements from local non-Christian initiation, marriage and burial rites—where these are capable of being adapted to Christian purposes. The underlying principle is understood to be a sacramental one.

Such a generalized document obscures, however, the extraordinarily varied problems of local incarnation which the geographic spread and cultural diversity of Christians present for liturgical worship. These emerge concretely in the studies of contemporary liturgical reform in the Anglican Communion gathered, along with some twenty new rites, in *Modern Anglican Liturgies 1958–1968*.[17]

The principle of diversity in worship was clearly articulated for the Anglican Communion in the time of Elizabeth I. Article XXXIV of the Thirty-nine Articles asserts that "traditions and ceremonies" need not be "in all places one and utterly alike," because they have always varied according to countries, times, and "men's manners." The criteria are spelled out in a straightforward manner: (1) traditions and ceremonies must not be contrary to God's word; (2) local church authorities have the right to establish such customs, and individuals must not go against duly established authority; and (3) the edification of the people should be the prime principle guiding those trying to decide what to change or abolish. Examples from three continents will show what difficulties confront local authorities trying to revise liturgies for the edification of their people today.

An Asian illustration comes from the Diocese of Hong Kong and Macao, where the Church faced cultural problems of concern to all Asian Christians, transcending the anomaly of "Chinese Anglicanism." A nineteenth century missionary bishop had wondered if it were necessary to use bread and wine in the Lord's Supper in a country which produces very little of either, and where rice-cakes and tea are the real equivalent to the Palestinian counterparts.[18] Since such a change would be contrary to God's Word, in the sense of the first criterion listed above, however, the contemporary reformers did not reopen this question.

Rather, they faced first the decision of what dialect to use, recognizing that whichever dialect they chose would appear to align the Church with one or another political and socio-economic position. Secondly, according to the report, they were particularly sensitive to the problem of ancestors in a Chinese cultural milieu. How can the prayers of the Church reflect the deep anxiety which some Chinese Christians feel about the departed, particularly those who were not Christian? A 1938 revision had framed a prayer with this local need in mind. A

1957 change had reverted to prayer only for the Church "militant here on earth"—thus using polemic language out of seventeenth century England less likely to speak to the condition of worshipers in Hong Kong.

Drums and beer, rather than tea and rice-cakes, define a ceremonial problem on African soil.[19] Efforts to introduce drums into worship apparently alienated some of the older African worshipers not because they associated drums with tribal religion, but because they linked them with modern beer halls. Some of the younger Africans liked the drums in church precisely for that reason; they spoke to secular society. And other young men approved of drums precisely because they did waken the religious depths of the old African culture.

Framers of a new "Liturgy for Africa," which originated in Uganda in 1964 and was subsequently approved for at least some trial use in the provinces of South and Central Africa, however, were not attempting to define ceremonial usage, just to establish a common text which could be duly translated into Swahili, Shona, Ndebele, Nyanja, Tswana, and other languages used by African worshipers. In spite of its title there is little in the "Liturgy for Africa" which reflects indigenous life. Simply because of its title, it was questioned both by Europeans living in Africa, and by African churchmen who suspected condescension. Experience with the "Liturgy for Africa" has led, it seems, to the wise if belated consensus that it would be well to wait for truly indigenous forms of worship to emerge from a culture; they cannot be given to it. Both in East Africa and in Nigeria, that decision has already been qualified to meet immediate demand for ecumenical forms. The Nigerians turned directly to the liturgy of the Church of South India for their model.

A South American form of indigenization is illustrated by the young Church in Chile.[20] In producing a 1967 experimental rite, the revisers grappled with three special Chilean problems. How was one to devise a single liturgy in modern Spanish for change-oriented, sophisticated city-dwellers and for semiliterate rural congregations? How was it possible to retain the best features of Anglicanism and yet come up with something not Anglo-Saxon in emotional tone but of truly Latin exuberance? How could they take account of Pentecostal worship so popular in Chile? They sought a kind of vigorous and robust worship, emphasizing the work of the Holy Spirit, which would leave open the doors to future reunion with the fast-growing indigenous Pentecostal churches.

That scandal of particularity which is always part of the Christian doctrine of the Incarnation is again evident, then, in the ways worship comes to be adapted to and in a given national ethos. These reports from three continents reveal, however, certain common supranational issues today. The generation gap in worship experience is not confined to Africa. The urban-rural problem is not confined to Chile. As they face these, Church leaders all over the world recognize that the reform of worship is an ecumenical concern, and cannot be undertaken unilaterally by any one tradition without regard for the reunion of Christians in that place.

North American Christians are apt to forget, when reading about changes in religious outlook "back" in the fourth century or "over" in Africa, that their own forms of worship and religious thought have undergone a similar process of indigenization in the past, and that new forms of worship must take account of the specifically American ethos. There is considerable evidence that our peculiar national perception of space is a major element in that ethos.

In *The Lively Experiment: The Shaping of Christianity in America,* Sidney E. Mead develops the thesis that space has overshadowed time in forming all the ideals most cherished by the American mind and spirit.[21] We equate freedom, for example, with unconfined movement in space. Practically unlimited space allowed our pioneer forefathers to escape the physical proximity of their neighbors. It allowed them always to "move on." And they moved into virgin space to find a new Eden.

Such a theory suggests that part of the crisis of the American spirit today comes from the radical change in our spatial environment. In a country growing crowded from sea to shining sea, most people can no longer find freedom in physical escape from their neighbors. And yet, Americans still express their freedom by moving about in space. Indeed, at an ever-increasing rate. Our great-grandfathers were considered well-traveled if they covered 30,000 miles in a lifetime. A business executive today, it has been estimated,[22] may easily fly three million miles in his lifetime. But an astronaut travels more than that in a week.

"Sacred space" in Christian worship appears to offer men both a boundary and a far horizon. It helps them define the local arena of action, where their neighbors live. It helps them also to look beyond and to move beyond the walls they build. This dual function is inherent in the framework of words and actions which the liturgy provides, and which elicits its own comprehension from those who accept this framework as their dwelling place.[23] We will try to trace the interwoven threads of these themes as we describe in the following chapters phenomena of touching and feeling, tasting and seeing which present themselves in Christian worship.

Chapter 8

TOUCH AND FEEL

WHEN on the first day of the week, Jesus came and stood among his disciples, he said to them: "Peace be with you." And when eight days later he came into their midst again, he said: "Peace be with you." Of the first occasion the report in John's Gospel notes, "the disciples were glad when they saw the Lord." Of the second it says that Jesus asked Thomas to touch his hands and to feel his side.

"Peace," the first word spoken by the Risen Lord to his gathered disciples in the Fourth Gospel tradition, is a word spoken in Christian worship with renewed frequency in our day. Along with it has come a notable effort to revive an ancient custom of expressing The Peace of the Lord not only with words but also through physical contact among all the worshipers by a handclasp or similar exchange of touch. Feelings, pro and con, have been so strong in many congregations that this act of touching warrants special attention in this chapter.

No handshake stands alone, however. The *Pax* belongs in the context of other phenomena of physical contact in worship, and in the perspective of contemporary thought about the meaning of such bodily interaction. Touching has an important role in the New Testament and in the worship which looks to the New Testament as its criterion. Christianity is not about intangibles.

Consider first that anatomical imagery with which biblical writers speak. Hands are instruments of creative power, of healing, of knowledge, and of fellowship. The anthropomorphic language of poetry permits the psalmist to speak of creation as the work of God's fingers (Ps. 8:3). The phrase is reminiscent of the second creation narrative in Genesis, particularly as it works in the imagination of a Jeremiah or a James Weldon Johnson. God is a potter whose hands mold our clay; he scoops up the stuff of earth and shapes it as a sculptor might. His "right hand" leads the Israelites out of bondage (Ps. 98:1); his "finger" writes his Torah for Moses to take to his people (Ex. 31:18). Steeped in this language in their worship, the earliest Christians thought of their risen Lord as standing at the right hand of God (Acts 7:55–56), the place not only of honor but, more especially, of power. His "hand" was with them as they preached the good news— and to this power many responded (Acts 11:21).

Luke's Gospel says that Jesus cast out demons "by the finger of God" (11:20). All of the gospels make much of the work of hands. Jesus stretches out his own hand to touch and heal a leper (Mk. 1:41). But he also commands a man who has a withered hand to stretch it forth: "he stretched it out, and his hand was restored" (Mk. 3:5). All who had diseases, it is said, pressed upon Jesus to touch him (Mk. 3:10). People kept bringing children to him that he might touch them (Mk. 10:13): "And he took them in his arms and blessed them, laying his hands upon them" (Mk. 10:16). His words and his deeds drew astonishment: "What is the wisdom given to him? What mighty works are wrought by his hands!" (Mk. 6:2).

The exclamation testifies not only to the Christian community's dual remembrance of what Jesus said and did, but also to the inseparability of word from act in all biblical thought. In the language of prayer in Acts 4:28–30, God's plan and his "hand" are interchangeable terms. The disciples' petition to speak his word with boldness is synonymous with the affirmation that he stretches out his hand to heal.

"What mighty works are wrought by his hands!" The exclamation also testifies to a culture which still had a lively sense of tactile powers. So a woman touches just the fringe of Jesus' garment and is healed; a man begs Jesus to come lay his hands on a sick child. So also when the author of the Apocalypse, in his vision on the Lord's Day, falls down in deadly fear, the Lord lays his right hand upon him saying: "Fear not . . ." (Rev. 1:17).

When the author of the first epistle of John wishes to stress the full reality of Christian experience, he insists that he is talking about that which they have not only heard and seen with their eyes, but "looked upon and touched with our hands" (1 Jn. 1:1). And when Paul wishes to describe the peaceful settlement of his differences with the leaders of the Jerusalem Church, he says that they gave to him and Barnabas "the right hand of fellowship" (Gal. 2:9).

The worship tradition of the later community attached special importance to two apostolic records of the laying on of hands with prayer. Act and word together express the intent of asking for God's gift of power to the persons on whom the hands are placed.

When the Twelve needed help in serving tables (and when they needed more Hellenists in the ministry, as the other strand of the narrative suggests), they chose seven men to whom they gave authority in this manner and for this purpose. Centuries later some churchmen came to use this account in Acts 6:1–6 as a New Testament warrant for their practices of ordaining men to special functions in the ministry of the Church of God through prayer accompanied by the apostolic touch.

When the Twelve heard that the Samaritans had been baptized without having received the Holy Spirit, they sent delegates, who prayed and then laid their hands upon them. The incident brought power to the Samaritans; its sequel explains the crime of simony (Acts 8:14–24). When Paul discovered disciples at Ephesus who had never even heard of the Holy Spirit (Acts 19:1–7), he laid his hands upon them and they received the Holy Spirit. These accounts provide later Christians with scriptural evidence that the act of Christian initiation is completed by the gift of the Holy Spirit through prayer and the laying on of hands.

As the Church spread out from the "Holy Land," all of these biblical precedents, with their tones and overtones, combined with existing cultural customs of touching. Tactual contact remained a regular feature of embodied Christian worship. It is especially noteworthy that some use of the hands is an explicit part of all seven of the sacramental rites in the Roman Catholic Church as these are described by Josef A. Jungmann. In the ancient rite of penance, for example, the period of public discipline was completed by a public act of reconciliation in which the bishop took the penitent by the hand, lifted him to his feet in the presence of the congregation, and returned him to full communion with the *Pax*.[1] In confirmation, to cite another example, the bishop still "performs the laying on of hands by anointing the forehead with chrism." He stretches his hand out over all the candidates collectively, as he prays for the sevenfold gifts of the Spirit. He also administers a light tap on the cheek of each.[2]

Hands play a similarly prominent role in the rites and ceremonies of the Episcopal Church as set forth in the Book of Common Prayer. To label these "manual acts" is technically correct, no doubt; but the Latinism obscures the everyday anatomy. Two occasions of touching in the Prayer Book services deserve special mention. Hands are more prominent than rings in the rubrics for matrimony: "The Minister, receiving the Woman at her father's or friend's hands, shall cause the Man with his right hand to take the Woman by her right hand. . . . Then shall the Minister join their right hands together, and say, 'Those whom God hath joined together. . . .'" The significance of their act is emphasized by his concluding words that the couple have declared their troth by giving and receiving a ring, "and by joining hands."

"Unction of the Sick" finds New Testament precedent in the account of what the Twelve said and did: "So they went out and preached that men should repent. And they cast out many demons, and anointed with oil many that were sick and healed them" (Mk. 6:12–13). Modern use of such anointings has aroused controversy among churchmen. The issues involved lie beyond the scope of this study; but the connection which the Prayer Book makes, both in the words of the prayer and in the rubric specifying conditions under which it is to be used, does not. If a sick person "in humble faith" asks for the ministry of healing "through Anointing or Laying on of Hands," the minister may use the prayer provided. It begins: "I anoint thee with oil (or I lay my hand upon thee), In the Name of the Father, and of the Son, and of the Holy Ghost. . . ."

Anointing with oil is another of the acts of touching and being touched in the history of Christian worship which carries with it a whole rainbow of associated meanings. It was, on the one hand, a quite ordinary part of taking a bath in ancient culture, if one could afford it—as indeed it still is for many people, under the same condition. The routine everyday connotation is best recaptured, perhaps, if one reads hand-cream or after-shave lotion in place of oil. The points to notice about such anointings in either case are their close connection with water, and with very basic (erotic, if you like) sensual satisfactions. But anointing with oil in the texture of biblical thought and biblical imagination also meant and means more than everyday care of the body. For, of course, The Anointed One is the king, the priest, the messiah—the Christ.

When, therefore, worshiping Christians through the centuries have rubbed oil on people or have been themselves anointed, they have intentionally invoked both levels of meaning. In the context of worship, ordinary human actions are imbued with extraordinary significance. Precisely because most Christians today do not classify anointing with oil as *a* sacrament, it is easier to ponder the adjective "sacramental" in this connection. The central point for earlier Christian worshipers, in all their debates with various advocates of "spiritual" religion through the centuries, was that God was truly incarnate in Jesus the Anointed One. In their worship in the name of, through, Jesus Christ, therefore, they were freed for thankful acknowledgment of their own embodiment. As whole persons they could and did respond in worship to the healing love of God demonstrated to them by the Lord who touched and was touched.

This understanding of Christian worship was summed up at the beginning of the third century by the theologian Tertullian in a pamphlet against Gnostics, and in defense of the resurrection of the flesh. It alludes to just those practices in the worship of his day which we have been talking about and will shortly make more specific: "The flesh is the hinge on which salvation depends. As a result, when the soul is dedicated to God, it is the flesh which actually makes it capable of such dedication. For surely the flesh is washed, that the soul may be cleansed; the flesh is anointed, that the soul may be consecrated; the flesh is sealed, that the soul too may be fortified; the flesh is shadowed by the imposition of hands, that the soul too may be illumined by the Spirit; the flesh feeds on the body and blood of Christ, that the soul as well may fatten. . . ." [3]

Tertullian is clearly presupposing that single but complex act of Christian initiation already described—an act which included washing and anointing and laying on of hands and Eucharist all in one. Not until Christian worshipers had practiced this act for half a millennium was it divided into three parts—Baptism, Confirmation, and Lord's Supper. The anointings which came to be linked with Confirmation were still part of the one initiation action in the fourth century, as they are today in some churches.

Bishop Cyril's lectures to the newly baptized in Jerusalem about 350 deal on successive days with Baptism, chrism, and the bread and wine of the Eucharist. Biblical evidence is adduced to show that the anointing they have received parallels

Christ's anointing with the Holy Spirit when he came up from the waters of the Jordan; Luke 4:18 is quoted: "The Spirit of the Lord is upon me; therefore the Lord hath anointed me; he hath sent me to bring good tidings to the poor." A careful distinction is drawn between Christ's anointing by the Father, and the Christian's anointing by men with material ointment, but nevertheless the ointment used after prayer for the Spirit is interpreted as not just ordinary ointment. It is, Cyril says, "the gift of Christ and of the Holy Spirit." It is a symbol of their having been made "partakers and associates of Christ." [4]

Some forty years later, Bishop Ambrose of Milan interprets the anointing in much the same way, though with even more flowery support from scripture, especially from the oil on Aaron's priestly beard (Ps. 133:2). He thus stresses more clearly the idea of the priesthood of all believers: "for we are all anointed by spiritual grace unto the kingdom of God and a priesthood." [5]

The tactile experience of early Christian initiation and its associated biblical symbolism, as both of these together were elaborated by the Fathers, included two more sensory references which should be noted. Fragrant oil came to be used, so that the sense of smell was involved; new white garments were donned. Ambrose can therefore give compressed expression to a host of interwoven impressions, and count on intelligent response from his listeners, by alluding in a single sentence to the love poetry of the Song of Solomon which the church of his day understood to be speaking allegorically of Christ and his Church: "How many souls regenerated today have loved thee, Lord Jesus, saying: 'Draw us after thee: we run after the fragrance of thy garments,' that they might drink in the odour of resurrection." [6]

Such a statement cannot be understood apart from the worship from which it is born and to which it addresses itself. Considered in that context, however, it is a fine example of a tactility broader than just the sense of touch through the skin. Marshall McLuhan has extended "tactility" to refer to the basic "interplay between all the senses, that functional ratio whereby reality is truly 'felt' and 'grasped.' " [7] Our common expressions "getting in touch" and "keeping in touch," McLuhan thinks, apply to this fruitful meeting of the senses which enables us to make sense of things.

In a perceptive theological reflection on "Marshall McLuhan's Theory of Sensory Form," W. Richard Comstock has applied this insight directly to worship. "It is clear that when sight, hearing, and the other senses are in tactile interaction, appropriate responses of adoration and commitment are possible," Comstock observes. "But if vision is heated up so that one 'stares' fixedly at the participants of the service, the worship event is immediately secularized into a lineal sequence of meaningless actions." [8]

Comstock's interpretation carries McLuhan's thought beyond the auditory emphasis we have already found in the earlier work, *The Gutenberg Galaxy*. He insists that McLuhan is recommending "the development of a dynamic tactile interplay among all the senses." [9] Just such "haptic harmony" appears to have been present in fourth century Christian worship as the bishops of Jerusalem and Milan understood it.

Other modern prophets besides McLuhan, however, are trying to restore man's wholeness of perception and experience. Two of them have particular relevance to phenomena of touching and being touched in worship. Rather than simply advocating it as a kind of inexpensive group therapy to promote "social adjustment," [10] they invite one to take with full theological seriousness the reality of man's body. In *Love's Body*, Norman O. Brown presents a new religious vision. In *The Human Metaphor*, Elizabeth Sewell recalls an old vision to new life.

Love's Body has been called a "breathtakingly beautiful piece of writing." [11] With its publication, its author is said to have emerged as "one of the most important religious thinkers of our time." [12] His style and the design of the book are the deliberate vehicles of the message. His aphorisms are intended to jolt his reader out of the reality principle which supposes that truth is achieved by abstract analysis. To try to recast

Brown's thought in discursive language is therefore necessarily to distort it. One must chew on the book itself. Nevertheless perhaps one can fairly point to four strands of his thinking which touch on our current topic.

First, Brown's program is one of breaking down walls. He rejects all of the split-level houses men build for their thinking and their living. This accounts in part for the fact that *Love's Body* goes beyond the Freudianism of his earlier work *Life Against Death;* psychoanalysis remained officially faithful to the reality principle whose pretensions it finally exposed.[13] Taking up from McLuhan a pregnant Yeats' image, Brown charges that the thinking man is in a "Lockean swoon." Philosophers talk as if man were "a winged cherub without a body," a pure knowing subject.[14] Phenomenologists would agree. The swoon also affects theatre-goers and church-goers. Contemporary liturgiologists would agree—since Brown specifies "liturgy, when participation consists in attendance at a spectacle. . . ." [15] Men are separated from one another and from themselves; separation on the outside is repression on the inside. And the root cause of all of this is man's split of self or soul from the body, for to divorce them is to take life from the body.

Secondly, Brown calls therefore for a rebirth of consciousness of ourselves as body. We need to construct "an erotic sense of reality." Such a new consciousness would be also a consciousness of symbolism, for symbolism is "mind making connections (correspondences) rather than distinctions (separations)." [16] Thus to become conscious of ourself as body would be to become conscious of mankind as One Body. Union is of bodies, not souls, Brown argues; Pope John, Freud, and Marx all shared one vision of the unification of mankind.

But thirdly, "everything is symbolic, everything including the human body." [17] We make our own bodies; our own images of the body. The body is not a thing, given and complete. It is plastic. This, says Brown, is the really revolutionary idea in psychoanalysis. The image of the body, the organization of the body can change: "What the psychoanalytically uninitiated call 'sex,' psychoanalysis calls 'genitality,' or 'genital organization,' seeing in it an arrangement, a *modus vivendi,* a political arrangement arrived at after stormy upheavals in the house of Oedipus." [18] This arrangement is not of natural necessity. It is merely the *status quo,* bearing the seal of the familiar.

What is needed, finally, is an apocalyptic breaking of that seal. To express his apocalyptic vision, Brown twice quotes a sentence from Northrop Frye's *Fearful Symmetry:* "The real apocalypse comes, not with the vision of a city or kingdom, which would still be external, but with the identification of the city and kingdom with one's own body.[19]

This idea of the body as the new temple comes clothed in many colors—Christian, Hindu, psychoanalytic, and Dionysian among them. Brown has meditated on such New Testament texts as "Do you not know that you are God's temple and that God's Spirit dwells in you?" (I Cor. 3:16); "Destroy this temple, and in three days I will raise it up. . . . But he spoke of the temple of his body" (John 2:19–21). With the help of Tertullian, Augustine, Jonathan Edwards, and a handful of more contemporary Christian writers, his chapter on "Fulfillment" issues an eschatological call: "The last thing to be realized is the incarnation . . . the body is of Christ." [20] Therefore, the true meaning of history is the bodily meaning. "Christ, the fulfillment, is not an abstract idea but a human body." [21] With the second coming of Christ, all flesh shall see it together—and there will follow a transition from passive identification to active participation in the mystical body.

Love's Body presents a powerful apocalyptic vision. On one level, it is a call for a Dionysian Christianity. At one point the alternative to dualism is seen to be "dialectics; that is to say, love. . . ." [22] But the book proceeds from dialectics toward Eastern monism. At one point Brown calls for resurrection from "history to mystery." [23] But the mysterious gives way to mysticism; the radically enigmatic is replaced by a mystical fusing of all things into One. Brown's aphorisms allow *mythos* finally to swallow *Logos,* the Dionysian to overwhelm Apollos. His vision nevertheless summons Christian worshipers to remove their "blinkers of decorum" in order to see the Word made flesh.

Logos remains in control of Elizabeth Sewell's poetic study, *The Human Metaphor.* When Locke fell into a swoon, the garden died. Man has creative work to do with his mind and his hands—shaping his own age, renewing the face of the earth. This is precisely what makes it imperative that he reexamine how he thinks about himself and his world: "Between us all, 'this world which is each man's work,' in Dylan Thomas's admirably traditional phrase, gets fashioned. Part of that making is the reciprocal influence of our methods of thought and our images of man. How we think . . . determines what we think we are." [24]

Miss Sewell's book has been fed by many of the same writings that inform the pages of *Love's Body.* Blake and Gerard Manley Hopkins, Coleridge and Owen Barfield; Freud and Norman O. Brown—the list could be extended. Their engagement with the mainstream of contemporary thought and their sense of urgency about the human situation are similar. *The Human Metaphor* also demands an end to disembodied thinking.

But it moves by another method and in an opposite direction from *Love's Body.* Instead of moving away from thought to the body, as Brown in effect invites us to do, *The Human Metaphor* moves from the body to thought. Although it says even less about touching and feeling as such, it offers three additional insights for our thinking about the topic. Miss Sewell's emphasis on the energy of metaphor in general, on anthropomorphic thought in particular, and on the poet Novalis, who stands behind Freud, are all relevant to the use of hands in worship.

Our divorce of body and mind has resulted, Elizabeth Sewell argues, in loss of power to think well. The Arrows of Intellect, in the phrase she borrows from Blake, must be reunited with the Arrows of Love if the human race is to get on with "the great communal work of being human." [25] We idolize THINK, but we conceive of the brain, of man himself, on the model of the machine. The abstraction has usurped the thinking power of the living organism in its fullness. The proper "ecological habitat" of thought is "our bodies first, our setting in the natural world, and the company of our fellowmen." [26] The inclusion of the last two members of this trinity is one of the major differences between Sewell's thought and Brown's. She knows it makes a difference what kind of garden one lives in. She is aware of the fact that Paul told the Corinthians that they (plural) were God's temple, with his Spirit *among* them.

Many scientists and poets, philosophers and priests, the argument continues, are rediscovering that when the phenomenal world is admitted to thought energy is created in the mind. Without the energy of metaphor, the brain cannot work properly.

One of the six common metaphors for nature which Miss Sewell explores to test her thesis of metaphoric productivity is the temple. It compares nature to a place, but not just a place—rather, "a place where something is going on." We will fail to feel the power of this metaphor in the poems, for example, of Beaudelaire, she says, if we conceive of a temple "merely as a place where people go to worship." None of the poets she cites uses it in this fashion: "They have, I daresay, a nobler and truer idea of what a temple, and worship, may be, for in this figure the temple is a place of intellectual striving, of discovery and effort, as indeed any true place of worship must be though we tend to forget this nowadays." [27]

Man discovers how to be human by working at it, Miss Sewell keeps suggesting. And man is a "mind-body organism working with its figures including itself." [28] To become a fully conscious mind-body with creative energy, man does not need only to learn language. He must also learn to love.

Unlike Brown, Sewell is in favor of making distinctions. As a working poet she is using "figure" or "metaphor" in a sense clearly distinguished from a psychological idea of symbols which are coughed up by the unconscious. We think with all our bodies including our sexual powers, she agrees; intelligence is indeed "diffused over the whole human frame." [29] But images of mental, emotional, or bodily states and happenings as the poet uses them are not just something to be decoded. They are "crossing-points" in a vast and flexible network of relations which man perceives for the purpose of interpreting himself and his world.

Everyman, says Miss Sewell, is a small poet. She is here in conscious agreement with phenomenological ideas about perception. The senses of the body do not record automatically and mechanically. They shape and build, "as if they were artists from the beginning." [30] We now know that our bodies "seeming so solid and well-skinned" are open to all sorts of influences "from love to fallout." [31] Human growth and activity depend on a marriage of man and environment. With this understanding of the dynamic interpenetration between "the universe within and without," she encourages a conscious reaffirmation of anthropomorphic thought. She finds all the great intellectual dynasties, both in arts and sciences, using three great metaphors of living intercourse between man and nature—all of them bodily. When the relation between them is figured forth as breathing, eating, or mating, she believes, the mind finds fruitful interpretative instruments for thought and work on behalf of our culture.

The split between mind and body has had especially suffocating effects on Christianity, Miss Sewell thinks. Since the Reformation, all Christianity "seems to have shut itself off by a *cordon sanitaire* from the erotic." [32] She calls on the young German Novalis—the eighteenth century poet whom Norman O. Brown had earlier recognized as a major influence on Freud's poetic thought—to restore Christian realism to our understanding of love, for the sake of everyman, for the sake of "squandering it abroad for the relief of the poor." [33]

Novalis, she finds, writes of erotic love "with an uncompulsive openness and friendliness unlike anyone else in modern times, seeing no reason to keep love and sex separate from his

deeply loved and simply held Christian beliefs. . . ." [34] Novalis found in his love for Sophie a universe of meaning match-
ing Dante's through his love for Beatrice. After Sophie died,
Novalis began the sacred songs which Miss Sewell draws on
to illustrate the celebration of love-and-death in terms both
human and divine. That is, in Christian terms. In his case, as
in Dante's, the physical phenomena of his own life were the
key which unlocked his mind to see the waters of a new country where "all that the touch of love made holy runs flowing
and free in . . . channels." [35] He goes on in the hymns to
see death as a call to a wedding, in the biblical figure of the
marriage feast of the Lamb.

The Human Metaphor thus leads one to recognize again
the mutual interaction between the embodied subject and his
world in worship. The focus of the book as of worship is not
just on poetry, but on life as it is invigorated by thought and
on thought as it is energized and made productive by life.
The book affirms in another metre the now familiar theses
that the human world is "the homeland of our thoughts" and
that our bodies are "the pivot of the world." [36] It also confirms the thesis that man's bodily existence is the principle of
his symbolizing, and that his symbolizing creates the possibility of grasping what he has experienced—in worship as
well as everywhere else.

St. Paul ends letters to the Corinthians and the Thessa-
lonians with the injunction: "Greet one another with a holy
kiss," or "Greet all the brethren with a holy kiss." The first
letter of Peter ends with the words: "Greet one another with
the kiss of love. Peace to all of you who belong to Christ."
The last words suggest already the meaning attached to the
greeting as it came to be used in worship by the time of Hippolytus; it was explicitly the act of baptized Christians.

The Apostolic Tradition specifies that catechumens shall
not give the kiss of peace "for their kiss is not yet pure. . . ."
The baptized are instructed to embrace one another, "men
with men and women with women." [37] In the Syrian liturgy
at the end of the fourth century, when the Peace was ex-

changed after the catechumens had been dismissed, the bishop greeted the congregation of the faithful with the words: "The peace of God be with you all." Then the deacon, using Paul's words, directed them to greet one another, and added, "and let the clergy kiss the bishop, the laymen the laymen, the women the women." [38]

Cyril of Jerusalem, in his commentary on the liturgy, is at pains to explain that the kiss is a reconciliation, not just the ordinary one friends use in greeting one another in public.[39] When employed by the faithful in the Eucharist, he insists, it is the same and yet not the same. It is a sign, he says, of forgiveness.

Contemporary interest in restoring an active use of the exchanged greeting among members of the congregation gained impetus from the Liturgy of the Church of South India, where the verbal greeting is accompanied by a form of handclasp adapted from an everyday public greeting, the equivalent in the Indian cultural context to the public embrace between friends in the culture of the Middle East. In Western culture the handshake appears to many to have a comparable status. Because every culture has what anthropologist Edward Hall calls its own "spatial accent," however, some Americans have found even this touch difficult to accept. They have been brought up, as Hall makes clear, in a space-ethos which discourages bodily contact. The normal interaction distance in many cultures is so different that people "cannot talk comfortably to one another unless they are very close to the distance that evokes either sexual or hostile feelings in the North American." [40]

Among the five major Protestant denominations whose recently revised liturgies propose a restoration of the Peace at the Lord's Supper, there are variations in the precise time and form of its use, but substantial agreement that it is a sign and symbol of the peace among Christians which is the gift of the Lord.[41] Some supporters urge it on these grounds, with special emphasis on being faithful to the biblical tradition and the ancient practice of the Church. Others support it not only because it is an appropriate expression of reconciliation among Christians, but also because it helps draw men out of their atomistic attitude toward worship, and out of their bottled-up attitude toward life. The latter emphasis links the Peace with all sorts of other experimentation with touch in worship.[42]

In the perspective of the ideas presented in this chapter, the use of hands-and-words together does have both historical precedent and contemporary relevance. Hands stretched out to one's neighbor in worship, however, would appear to be an act of even greater meaning and potency than partisans of the *Pax* usually recognize. As Norman O. Brown's Dionysian vision leads us to see, it is a way of breaking down walls in ourselves and between ourselves, to come out of doors into the reality of our incarnation and of the Incarnation. As Elizabeth Sewell's Apollonian tapestry leads us to see, it is also one way of ordering, forming, and energizing our thinking, that we may be transformed by the renewing of our minds for the work of renewing the world.

By their respective brands of symbolic logic, both modern prophets would lead worshipers to expect to feel again in the neighbor's hand, the touch of the hand of the Lord upon them, and to learn from it to reach out in turn to other men in the name of the Lord.

Chapter 9

ARCHITECTURAL SPACES

JUST AS our experience of chronology today is organized around weekends, annual vacations, and retirement, so our everyday experience of geography is organized around our dwelling places, our cities, and our nations. And just as Christian worship offers man new meanings for those intervals in his calendar, so Christian worship offers him comparable significance for the concentric circles of his social space.

The natural landscape has faded as far into the background of our environment as have the temporal cycles of nature. Mountains and forests and caves—once the sites of awe and worship—have lost much of their mysterious power over man's life. Christian faith, as we said in the last chapter, sees the human community itself as the new temple, the sacred precinct of God's dwelling place with men. Nevertheless it has never abandoned the idea of other temples, other sanctuaries cut off or hedged about with spatial significance. In this chapter we shall think about the role of three major spaces—beginning with the household, which is for Christian space what Sunday is for Christian time.

Christian scripture and tradition state unequivocally that the God whom "the heaven of heavens cannot contain" cannot be localized in a temple made by hands. Yet even those who would denounce as rank superstition the notion that the deity dwells in buildings, acquiesce in popular practice. Any Saturday newspaper in the country will gladly direct you to half a dozen Houses of God. One aspect of the liturgical revival in the twentieth century, the logical corollary of renewed emphasis on the Church as the People of God, is a renewed sense of the church building not as the house of God, but rather as the house of God's *people*.

The house-church is the most prominent place of worship in the New Testament, both in practice and in theory. We even know the names of some of those first century Christians whose homes were large enough to serve as places of assembly. Aquila and Prisca "together with the church in their house" in Ephesus sent greetings through Paul to the Christians at Corinth (I Cor. 16:19). Paul sent his special greetings to Nympha "and the church in her house" at Laodicea (Col. 4:16). Philemon (the man to whom Paul wrote that moving personal appeal so often overlooked among his letters) had a church in his house in neighboring Colossae. Nor was house-centered worship limited to an infant institution. Excavations at Dura-Europus have shown that Christians were using a remodeled house for worship there as late as 232.[1]

The Church in the New Testament is always identified with people before places. Because those people assembled for worship in houses, however, they thought of their community in household terms. The Jerusalem Bible has emphasized the first point by translating two of Paul's uses of *ekklesia*, which the RSV renders *church*, with the alternative word *community* (I Cor. 11:18, 22). But it has obscured the latter point by using the word "brothers" in place of Paul's use of "household" of faith (Gal. 5:10). Households then and now contain more complex human relationships than fraternities. The "household of faith" in Pauline language becomes "household of God" in Petrine language (I Peter 4:17), and it is with members of that household that judgment is said to begin.

Both a sense of present judgment on the household of God and a sense of the functional simplicity of New Testament house-churches appear to be at work among Christian worshipers today. Some of them conclude that the day of the church building is over. They cannot justify spending more than a billion dollars a year for church construction programs in America alone. Furthermore, they welcome the intimacy, the informality, the sense of being a household which worship in someone's living room or dining room or kitchen once again affords. Hence there is an appreciable movement away from the church building. It is agreed in principle that for the Lord's Supper, "a moderately large, well-proportioned room is needed, in its center a table and on the table a bowl of bread and a cup of wine . . . that is all." [2]

That judgment was made, however, by a leading liturgical architect. It represents also the attitude of those who favor building new churches and renovating old ones to promote maximum understanding of Christian worship as the action of the household of God. Fully active participation of the Christian community in the public work of worship, these defenders of special assembly halls argue, is scarcely possible in the limited space available in most modern homes. At least for Sundays, a larger space is needed in which Christians can gather together to be formed as, and to give visible expression to, the *ekklesia* of God in a given location.

In designing such assembly halls, the modern liturgical architect is aware that action generates space. If the organization of space called church architecture is to be generated out of a dynamic, energetic concept of worship, it must be more than a mere enclosure. As one architect puts it: "Of all buildings, the church building must be the sort which says to the people who gather, 'You are the important things here. You are the temple of God. I am not.' The nature of the shelter in its scale, its light, color, texture, and space must be lovingly subservient to the community of persons it shelters." [3] He understands his task as one of ordering space in response to the logic of the liturgy. Since people move in liturgy, their movements imply certain configurations of space. And, as he sees it, the old ideas of nave, choir, and sanctuary are spa tially irrelevant in a church which will best reflect and encourage common participation.[4]

It is easier to define the problem in these terms than to solve it. A fundamental issue confronts those who would translate the logic of the liturgy into spatial relations. The eucharistic liturgy, as the ecumenical church so widely recognizes, has two foci of action. The household assembles to share together the Ministry of the Word and the Ministry of the Lord's Supper. When a church is focused around the table or altar, the space for reading and proclaiming the Word appears to be less important. Conversely, when the place of reading and preaching is duly emphasized, it is more difficult to convey the space of the shared meal. Very few liturgical-minded Christians today would defend the design of those Protestant churches which put an elevated pulpit front and center, but most of them would admit that the human ear is so designed that it hears better sounds coming from in front.

Some Christians still want to make one or the other focus dominant. A Roman Catholic writer, for example, says quite simply that the Christian church is a dining hall, and that we must explore the situation which best befits meal behavior.[5] A Protestant Christian betrays the other ideal when he praises "the congregation gathered around the pulpit," [6] on the model of ancient synagogues where the faithful gathered round the reading desk from which the Divine Word sounded forth.

More typically, present thinking about the Word and the Sacrament demands a space of worship so organized that it will somehow equalize both foci. Thus another Roman Catholic writer responds with enthusiasm to a principle stated in an appendix to the chapter on sacred art and sacred furnishings in the Constitution on the Sacred Liturgy. It directs that "in building churches, the ambos or lecterns for the sacred readings should be so arranged that the dignity and honor of the Sacred Scriptures and of the proclamation of the Word of God itself will be immediately apparent." [7] He interprets this statement to mean that the ambo or lectern should be on the same axis as the altar. His rationale is worth attention: "The

Mass consists of two integrally related parts, the liturgy of the Word, and the eucharistic liturgy; we are invited to join in the table of the Word and the table of the eucharistic bread. For not from bread alone does man live, not even the bread of Christ's body, but from every word that proceeds from the mouth of God. And undoubtedly most significant of all, is the document's declaration that Christ '*is present in his Word,* since it is he himself who speaks when the holy scriptures are read in the Church.' " [8]

Thus also, and with similar enthusiasm, a Calvinist writing on liturgical architecture supports the idea put forth by Karl Barth in 1959. Worshipers, Barth said, should gather around a simple wooden table fitted with a removable lectern, so that it can serve at one and the same time as pulpit and communion table. [9]

Both of these writers are working from an idea of the Church and its action in worship determined by domestic imagery of the household of God. Hence both reject the traditional idea of an elongated space of worship.

The Roman Catholic believes that if one abandoned all preconceived notions of church architecture and proceeded from the essential action-structure of the Eucharist, one could come up "with an architectural space of almost any conceivable shape and form *except* the long rectangular shape we have inherited." [10] The Protestant argues firmly and in polemic tones for the circle as such. Both the square spaces and the elongated spaces which were delimited for worship from Constantine to the Reformation are "perversions," as he sees it, of the true Christian spatial form. There must be a circular "convergent" arrangement of worshipers, so that they can have visible face-to-face encounter with their neighbors. When the table stands among a people who are the household of God, "the place of worship gives visible expression of the event which creates the Christian church." [11] For the community is gathered by the Lord Jesus around the holy table to hear his Word and to respond with mutual upbuilding in love.

Although the circle may thus seem to some to be the spatial environment best suited to the essential action of the liturgy, it is subject to three major criticisms. In the first place, a circular plan fails to show that the members of the household do not all have the same function, and it often fails to provide adequate space for the special ministers to function in. In the second place, it overemphasizes the interior to the neglect of the outside community. In the third place, it creates too cozy a domestic scene, one which can smother the equally important New Testament and liturgical motif of a people on the march.

The Anglican Peter Hammond, one of those making the first criticism, uses a musical analogy: the Eucharist resembles a polyphonic motet rather than a plainsong melody. The spatial relationships must similarly express separation and identity between nave and sanctuary.[12] The ancient house-church arrangement was such that the celebrant of the feast, the leader of the assembly, sat behind the table, flanked by his assistants. The ancient basilica provided for diversity of function in a comparable way, with chairs in the apse for bishop and presbyters. Hence some post-conciliar Roman Catholics speak of integrating "the three poles of the liturgy (chair, pulpit, altar)." [13]

This first criticism is made by those who are primarily concerned to stress the domestic setting of Christian worship, however. Reflection on the second criticism leads out of the house to the city. Reflection on the third leads forward to the place of the Kingdom in Christian worship.

"The Great Intercession" is considered an essential feature of the full eucharistic rite. In the experimental Order of Worship recommended to the churches by the Consultation on Church Union, it comes after the exchange of the Peace; it includes petitions for the peace of the whole world, for all on whose labor the worshipers depend, for all who suffer, for the community in which the worshipers live. In the early Church such Prayers of the Faithful followed the dismissal of the catechumens and preceded the Offertory. They were, that is, an act only of those fully initiated into Christ, but also an act to which they gave first priority.

Since the intercession was part of what was done in secret, Justin Martyr felt obliged to explain these prayers in his second century efforts to prove to the Romans that Christian worship was not a subversive activity. The faithful pray, he says, not only for themselves but "for all other persons wherever they may be, in order that . . . we may be deemed fit through our actions to be esteemed as good citizens. . . ." [14]

If the setting of worship is to be derived from the logic of the liturgical action, it would seem that it must somehow include the logic of the Great Intercession. If the Christian is called in worship to such civic work, the church building must express and evoke this relationship. The secular city creates new spatial demands on the ecclesiastical architect because it creates new spatial perception in the human beings who assemble for worship.

Looked at just from the outside, the old village church and the new one near the suburban shopping center, appear to be equally irrelevant to the city. It is easy to romanticize the past, of course; and so any tourist in rural England or New England gets a picture of tower or steeple defining the community. When every ear in town could hear the churchbell, we like to think, or every eye look up at the cross or rooster linking heaven and earth, men who were invited to pray "for the whole state of Christ's Church" knew the full dimensions of that task.

It is almost as easy to romanticize the present. The skyline along America's freeways and byways is cut by "butterfly roofs, peaks and planes with knifelike edges, miniature ski jumps and concoctions of folded and scalloped concrete" [15] —and everyone driving by recognizes a new church, whether or not he has time to see the imposing sign at the entrance. If churchmen have thought of their building programs as a missionary strategy, they are having second thoughts: "Thus we cast our net of stone, wood, and glass before the neighborhood and hope that the unwary may be trapped," one sharp critic has observed; "the trouble is that the wary and unwary are a few blocks away on another, less attractive street, suffering, simply staying alive. . . ." [16]

Looked at from the inside, as it were, the walls and windows around worshipers, and most especially the entrances and exits, share the function of defining the Christian's dual citizenship. The ancient tale of two cities is assuming new vitality for worshipers today, whether they live physically in the middle or on the edges of the urban crisis. To explore the old geopolitical imagery in order to see its relevance to the environment of the community, we must go first to Jerusalem, the center of the world, the City of God.

Historians of religions have fully established the ubiquity of center symbolism in religious thinking. In various forms appearing over and over again, the place of worship is conceived as the center of the earth. Thus Apollo's temple at Delphi represented the omphalos or navel of the world to ancient Greek worshipers. The associated myth had it that Zeus, when he wanted to find the center of the earth, set two birds free, one to fly east and one to fly west. They met at Delphi. Both are represented on the sculptured stone omphalos which has been discovered there. Strabo adds cannily that the place was almost in the center of Greece. [17]

This Hellenic occurrence is a good example of the kind of evidence from all over the world from which Mircea Eliade concludes that every culture has a sacred mountain situated at the center of the earth, where heaven and earth meet; and that every temple becomes a "sacred mountain" and hence the center, the *axis mundi,* the meeting point of heaven, earth, and hell. [18]

So it was at Jerusalem. The omphalos myth was known to the ancient inhabitants of Jerusalem before David captured the city. Although it was foreign to ancient Yahwism, it subsequently had great influence on temple circles in the capital city. [19] The biblical echoes are numerous and complicated.

The mythic concept clearly lies behind the great vision in

Isaiah 2:2–4 when all nations flow to the mountain of the house of the Lord to beat swords into plowshares. It informs the pages of Ezekiel; it recurs many times in the apocryphal literature, as in the Wisdom of Solomon 9:8. In the New Testament, its imaginative power shapes Luke's theology of history, beginning from and returning to Jerusalem. It certainly determined the powerful symbolism of Paul's collection for the saints, and it probably determined as well his understanding of his whole missionary journey.

With all the weight of this tradition behind it, the holy city, the new Jerusalem, descends from heaven in the penultimate chapter of the Bible, to epitomize the new heaven and the new earth. Its walls and streets and open gates are described in great detail, for in this city no temple is needed. All of its citizens worship the One whose throne is in its midst.

This highly political imagery has never lost its power over the Christian imagination. It accounts in part for the phenomenon of the Crusades; the idea of freeing Jerusalem merged in the Crusaders' consciousness with the spatial eschatology of the gathering of all nations about Jerusalem, the center of the world.[20] It accounts for much of the architectural symbolism of the medieval cathedral which was thought of as representing the celestial Jerusalem.[21] And it is heard in our day in Christian hymns and from Christian Councils: "In the earthly liturgy we take part in a foretaste of that heavenly liturgy which is celebrated in the holy city of Jerusalem towards which we journey as pilgrims. . . ."[22]

The sixth century geometer Anthemius managed to give consummate spatial expression to this concept in designing Hagia Sophia, the great Church of Christ as the Holy Wisdom of God. Even a modern tourist in Istanbul experiences a "floated in-between world." [23] Worshipers moving down the immensely long processional axis under the swelling canopy of the vast dome must have known that they were at that center where earth and heaven meet. But Byzantium is as remote from most modern urban life as the holy city of Jerusalem. Can a twentieth century Christian make any sense out of the image of the City of God in the space of his worship?

Only, it would seem, if he juxtaposes it with the City of Man —both in imagination and in liturgical act and architecture. No one wants another attempt to build Jerusalem through a Gothic Revival. There are too many signs that the tension between Jerusalem and—Hoboken, let us say, is properly disturbing Christian worshipers today. Light of a "heavenly city" illuminates for them the dark city streets to which they return from the spaces of worship, only insofar as they bring into worship the spaces through which they have traveled on the way.

On one level, such a statement is another expression of the metaphoric tension evoked by the spatial language of worship. As we have said time and again, this language serves to energize worshipers for action in and beyond the liturgical assembly. Thus when a contemporary professor of poetry questions the delimited three-dimensional language of the City, he notes with delight that Pope John's call to open the windows of the Church was issued from St. Paul's-Outside-the-Walls.[24] But he also concludes that the walls and gates built into the urban imagery are essential for the Christian life. The Church's orientation is different from the world's.

The tale of two cities addresses the Christian person with a language of limit which is also the language of witness. In this sense, the image of the City of God becomes an image of hope for the City of Man, a call to a public act of imagination which will proceed beyond fantasy to restructuring reality.[25] Christian worshipers believe, with Augustine, that the two cities are ever mixed, inside as well as outside of church buildings. Judgment belongs to God. Confession belongs in worship.

On another level, therefore, many would urge the architect to translate the metaphor of two cities into his language of space. They want, for a start, to eliminate the subdued "night-club" lighting of churches, for the sake of "a new quality of space that is conducive to community action." [26] They want to arrange furnishings and worshipers so that the latter look beyond each other. The full problem is obviously far from a simple one. No tricks will accomplish it, surely; but it is doubtful whether a plain brick box will either—however redolent of hospitality inside. Both architectural and theological seriousness are called for, if the space of worship is to be one which presses outward from the center, not in the form of a monument in technopolis but in spatial dialogue with the surrounding human community.

The challenge to the architect is to express in light and space a boundary which, in Romano Guardini's words, is like our skin—one which breathes and feels and transfers from one side to the other.[27] The human analogy is inescapable because in Christian worship Christ is the center of the new city, but his love has no circumference.

The third major criticism of programs to determine the space of worship solely on the model of the house-church, we said earlier, is that it tends to counteract the idea of a pilgrim church. It invites the false equation that the Church at worship is the Kingdom of God. The criticism clearly has both a theological presupposition and an architectural consequence.

Jean-Philippe Ramseyer of the Taizé Community has made this criticism forcibly in his book, *La Parole et l'image,* written to encourage dialogue within an ecumenical perspective between the Church and artists. He answers the plea for a circular arrangement of space, setting worshipers face to face, with a telling statement drawn from Saint-Exupéry: "To love it is necessary to look together in the same direction." [28]

Believing that all plastic expression must conform to the event of which it is an image, furthermore, Ramseyer reminds students of Christian architecture not only of the Resurrection but of the Kingdom yet to come. Ecclesiastical space must be shaped, he thinks, to express a community on the move toward this future. The very fact of a building, a delimited space, expresses the "already" of the Kingdom here and now. Somehow it must be so arranged as to express also the "not-yet"—the dynamic of the forward march.

For this theological reason, Ramseyer proposes a longitudinal axis, a space of worship akin to the shape of a bus. He sees the proclamation of the Word as the stimulus to the journey, but notes most sensibly that it is therefore inappropriate to put the pulpit in the middle of the road. By the same token, the table is not the end of the journey either, as he sees it, but rather a station *en route*.[29] Therefore he thinks it must always have a space behind it, in order to place worshipers before the mystery of the Kingdom yet to come, reminding them of that which separates the Church from its ultimate goal and End.

The analogy of the bus is beautifully mobile and modern; but the elongated space which it proposes is precisely that of the long nave which dominated Western ecclesiastical architecture from the fourth century through the Middle Ages. One might observe that the word *nave* derives from the Latin for ship, to which the church was likened. Although ships were also presumably vehicles of movement from place to place, it became customary to stress, rather, the safety of the ship over against the storm-tossed world outside. Numerous biblical narratives were used to illustrate such interpretation, especially that of Noah's ark. One could enter the nave and be safe from the flood. The oblong shape derives from the *basilica,* which originally meant an imperial palace but came to mean any public assembly hall in the Graeco-Roman world. It is worth noting also that basilica and *basileia,* the New Testament word for the Kingdom, are cognate.

Far more important than verbal associations with names and parts of buildings, however, is the quality of the lived space of worship which the building creates. Every spatial environment encourages some actions and discourages others. In the civic basilicas of imperial Rome, processions were a natural. The Christians who copied the shape of these buildings began also to develop ceremonial processions as part of their regular cultic action. In fact, along with this type of building, according to Schmemann, "a complex system of entrances, exits and litanies, of the movement of the whole praying congregation from one place to another, was introduced into worship, and this of course gave to worship not only an inner but also an outer dynamic, a dramatic and symbolic significance." [30]

If the phenomenological understanding of man's wholeness is taken seriously, one cannot accept this implication that inner dynamism can be sustained without an outer dynamic. Schmemann seems to ignore the fact that "man has a physical, spatio-temporal, bodily existence, even in matters of salvation." [31] It follows, it seems to me, that a space conducive to processions is for that very reason conducive also to the forward movement of a pilgrim church which distinguishes its own assembly from the Kingdom of God. A community can, certainly, move forward, have a procession, without imperial pomp. That being admitted, the very innovations which Schmemann blames for a decline of primitive eschatological understanding would seem, rather, to evoke and express it.

When one thinks of the spaces of worship in relation to the Kingdom of God, however, it is essential to remember that the Kingdom of which the New Testament speaks is not a place, not a limited area of dominion. It is, rather, the Reign of God. In insisting on a distinction between the Church and the Kingdom, Christians insist also on avoiding dissociation between them. The post-Easter Church believed that with the Resurrection of Christ the Reign of God had become "decisively operative" [32] in their midst. In the time between the Resurrection and the Parousia, the Church lives to serve the Reign of God. It prays for the coming consummation of his Kingdom. As Hans Küng has put it sharply, it prays not "Let us realize thy kingdom!" but "Thy Kingdom come!" [33] Yet it also celebrates the Lord's Supper, which proclaims and represents the eschatological meal in that Kingdom.

To that eating and drinking we must now turn. Yet the dialectic we have just acknowledged between the community which is directed toward, and at the same time already belongs to, the coming Kingdom, presents a further challenge to those who shape the space of Christian worship. It demands that the church building present in concrete forms of space and substance a mystery beyond space. But that, as artists understand, is one function of art—to open a gate to the numinous. Through such a gate Christian worshipers look beyond political boundaries for the healing of the nations.

Chapter 10

TASTE AND SEE

"O taste and see that the Lord is good!" (Ps. 34:8). Human eating is always something more than a way to satisfy physical hunger. People respond to the taste and the texture, the smell and the sight of their food—and with several layers of consciousness. Any meal, especially when two or three are gathered together to share it, is a complicated affair, a ritual act. When it is a festive meal, a celebration, it grows even more complex. A feast invariably becomes a deliberately symbolic act, a conscious ritual of human interaction. The full Christian liturgy is such a feast; at its climax people eat and drink together. We will explore in this chapter some dimensions of that feast, in the web of intentions which give it distinctive meaning in Christian worship.

Food and drink are powerful symbols in our lives and hence in all religions because they are never unambiguous. Food and drink not only sustain life; they can also poison us. All men are attracted to some foods and repelled by others. Our taste buds account directly for some of this, and all languages expand upon their response to what is bitter as well as to what is sweet. The Bible speaks of "tasting" the goodness and kindness of the Lord; it speaks also of "tasting" death.

When we consider our own food likes and dislikes, however, we realize that they result in large part from our cultural training, and from our family and personal histories. The eye of a

141

sheep may be a great delicacy to the Bedouin, but a horror to most Europeans. Although a slab of rare beef may never taste quite the same after one has read Gandhi's autobiography, it is a treat for most Americans; it is repulsive to most Indians. Functional allergies to broccoli or Spam can be our response to a college or army experience *in toto*. Watermelon may always taste happily of the Fourth of July, creamed onions of Thanksgiving, and cocoa of camping trips—even to people who do not much like the actual flavor of any of them. "Soul food" is not known only in the black community.

What we eat evidently gets its symbolic value more from its social context than from our body chemistry. Historically, the Christian family has given symbolic value to several foodstuffs in its worship. Since in apostolic times the Eucharist was celebrated in the context of a full meal, it is not surprising to find fish on the menu in the Synoptic accounts of Jesus feeding the multitudes, and in the Fourth Gospel's account of his post-Resurrection sharing of bread and fish with his friends by the Sea of Galilee. All of these accounts as we have them were influenced by retelling in the worship of the early community. Because of the acrostic found in the Greek ICHTHUS, moreover, the fish came to stand for the Lord himself. One early Christian recorded the fact that when he visited Rome they set before him in worship "for food the fish from the spring." [1]

Although there is no evidence that fish was literally a part of the eucharistic meal as late as the year 200, gifts of cheese and olives were still brought to the eucharistic assembly at that time. The Rite of Hippolytus provides special prayers for blessing these offerings, with such words as "Grant also that this fruit of the olive depart not from thy sweetness, [this fruit] which is the type of thy fatness which Thou hast caused to flow from the Tree for the life of them that hope in Thee." [2] Such a prayer catches up the New Testament imagery which links the tree of the cross on which Jesus was hanged with the ancient Tree of Life symbol, and both of them with the olive tree which provided a staple of the Mediterranean diet. The cheese and olives so blessed were later distributed to the poor.

Similarly, milk and honey had a place in the initiation rites at that time. At their first Eucharist, the newly baptized were offered three sips from a cup of milk sweetened with honey. Tertullian calls this "a foretaste of peace and fellowship." [3] The symbolic connection with the biblical "Promised Land" flowing with milk and honey is obvious. So also are the connections with infancy. This practice in Christian worship may already have been in the minds of the authors of Hebrews and I Peter, giving extra force to their words about milk *versus* solid food (Heb. 5:12), and about growing up to salvation by longing for pure spiritual milk (I Pet. 2:2). It may also be in St. Paul's mind when he tells the Corinthians that he had to feed them with milk because they were still "babes in Christ" (I Cor. 3:2).

From the beginning, however, bread and wine were the food and drink which had a special claim on the Christian palate; and both of them have proved inexhaustibly rich symbols to this day. Although bread and wine take their full meaning from the context in which they appear, it will be helpful to note first some of their special properties in themselves, since these have been obscured in contemporary worship. Many Christians substitute for bread, insubstantial and virtually tasteless individual wafers; others replace a cup of wine mixed with water, with miniature individual containers of grape juice.

Bread eaten in the worship of the early Church was the bread also eaten at home. Its everydayness was an integral part of its symbolism in the Eucharist. It tasted like everyday bread, as Cyril of Jerusalem maintained; one even had to consider the crumbs.[4] It was assimilated and it nourished one, as Justin Martyr declared.[5] Only because they started from the presupposition of good solid food, were the Fathers able to develop their ideas of the spiritual strength and sustenance which the worshiper received from eating this common bread made uncommon in the Eucharist. They could thus link it with the petition for bread in the Lord's Prayer. They could let their imagination play upon the whole intricate process whereby man's work and God's bounty resulted in the loaf about to be broken and shared. Even though Jesus' Last Supper with his disciples may have required the unleavened bread appropriate to Passover, there was no emphasis on historical imitation in this detail until the eighth century, when unleavened bread came to be used in the West.

Contemporary Christians are again emphasizing the use of a loaf or loaves of good solid bread, not only to make clearer one of the essential actions of the meal, but also to help regain some of the natural, straightforward thanksgiving for food which was part of the primitive Eucharist. Christian prayer at that meal has intimate connections with the Jewish blessing, which was part of every supper in first century Palestine: "Blessed art thou, Lord God, King of the Universe, who bringest forth bread from the earth."

A remnant of eating bread in this reverent freedom is visible at the conclusion of the Greek Orthodox liturgy today when worshipers leave the church munching on pieces of blessed bread. This food is distinguished from the consecrated bread of the Eucharist, however. It is said to denote brotherhood in Christ, and interpreted as reminiscent of the early Agape, considered as a separate event.

The Cup in the worship of the early Church contained wine mixed with water. The common cup was taken for granted in early thinking about this sacrament, as it was in the words of Jesus repeated in the eucharistic prayer. The mixture of the wine and water was also considered important by early commentators. Cyprian of Carthage explains it as a symbol of the union between Christ and the Church; the water represents the people and the wine the blood of Christ. He protested vehemently that the fruit of the vine is indispensable: "For when Christ says, 'I am the true vine,' the Blood of Christ is, indeed, not water, but wine." [6]

Some Christians in Africa were using only water in the Cup in Cyprian's day. He suspects that it is not just because they are rigorists who object to the use of alcoholic beverages, but because they are afraid of persecution if the smell of wine is detected on their breath in the morning. It would betray the fact that they had participated in the forbidden early morning services. Furthermore, Cyprian writes to a fellow bishop, unless wine is used, the worshipers cannot see Christ's blood in the chalice.

Such a letter not only shows "realism" about the theological meaning of the sacrament in the third century, as theologians like to point out; but also refreshing realism about drinking wine. Cyprian even includes the report of Noah's being drunk (Gen. 9:20) among the Old Testament texts about wine which he collects to show that the mixed cup is "according to the scriptures." A similar realism lies behind St. Ambrose's comments on the Cup. His Latin text of Psalm 23 read "my cup inebriates" instead of "my cup overflows." Ambrose quotes this psalm as pointing to the Eucharist. He also repeats the saying of another psalmist that wine "maketh glad the heart of man." [7]

The whole psalm of praise and thanksgiving for creation, from which the last quotation comes, expresses one element always associated with eating and drinking in Christian worship, especially the lines:

> Thou dost cause the grass to grow for the cattle,
>   and plants for man to cultivate,
> that he may bring forth food from the earth,
>   and wine to gladden the heart of man,
> oil to make his face shine,
>   and bread to strengthen man's heart.
> —*Psalm 104:14–15*

Bread for strength and wine for gladness suggest, indeed, the same duality of order and ecstasy which we have observed in other phenomena of Christian worship. The eucharistic prayer of the Didache goes on to indicate the additional Christian meaning of this food and drink, but it has retained clearly this continuing element of making eucharist: "Thou, Lord Almighty, hast created all things for the sake of Thy name and hast given food and drink for men to enjoy, that they may give thanks to Thee. . . ." [8]

The similarities between any family meal and the pattern of the family meal in the context of Christian worship have been keenly observed and beautifully described by the modern American writer James Agee. As he watches breakfast preparations in a southern mountain cabin, he remembers his experience as a schoolboy getting up "through the cold lucid water of the Cumberland morning and to serve at the altar of earliest lonely Mass, whose words were thrilling brooks of music and whose motions, a grave dance." [9] He sees this grave dance re-enacted: "It is in no beauty less that the gestures of a day here begin: and in just such silence and solitude: the iron lids are lifted: the kindling is laid in the grate: and the lids replaced: and a squirting match applied beneath: and the flour is sifted through shaken window screen . . . all these things with set motions, progressions, routines and retracings of bare feet and of sticklike arms, stick hands, contractions of the sharp body: . . . the biscuits tan, the eggs ready, the coffee ready, the meat ready, the breakfast ready . . . on this food must be climbed the ardent and steep hill of the morning." [10]

Precisely this quality of vision informs, it seems to me, the description of the Christian meal which Dom Gregory Dix develops with scholarly fullness in his influential book of twenty-five years ago, *The Shape of the Liturgy*. "Worship," Dix wrote in the introduction, "is a mysterious but also a very direct and commonplace human activity. It is meant for the plain man to do, to whom it is an intimate and sacred but none the less quite workaday affair." [11]

Since publication of Dix's study, liturgical scholarship has advanced to the point where many details of the work are no longer accepted; but students remain indebted to his clear perception of a fourfold action in the liturgical tradition of the Christian Church. The model is not the Last Supper as such, which had seven actions in the New Testament accounts, but a simplification of these. The table is set. Thanks is given. The bread is broken. The meal is eaten. These basic actions of daily human life become the offertory, consecration, fraction, and communion of the Lord's Supper.

Each of these four actions has been the subject of a vast literature—theological, historical, pastoral, and devotional. Each has also been the subject of different interpretations in different parts of the Christian family. The sense of simplicity and naturalness which Agee and Dix both suggest, however, is reflected in contemporary liturgies.

Even as the preparation of any meal is both functional and expressive, it is believed, so it should be in the context of worship. The early Christian worshipers brought food from home —small loaves of bread and small containers of wine. In Rome as late as the era of Gregory the Great, the clergy went around among the people at the time of the offertory to collect these gifts. The bread was put in linen bags held by the deacons; the wine was poured into a common container.[12] In other places, the people put their bread gifts into baskets as they arrived, and these were carried to the table when the time came. The point now newly re-emphasized is that these gifts represent the worshipers' ordinary lives and work. The preparation, setting the table, is the action of the people. They and their representatives should take an active part in getting ready for the meal.

Once the bread and wine are ready, the action of giving thanks is expressed in the prayer that follows. Indeed, this prayer (the *anaphora* or *canon*) is said to have the function of expressing the meaning of the whole rite.[13] Each word of the eucharistic prayers known from the great liturgies of East and West has therefore been scrutinized, analyzed, and weighed with exhaustive care by theologians and liturgiologists. It would be impossible to review this work here in sufficient detail to do justice to its seriousness in Christian thought. But three summary comments are called for.

First, many ordinary worshipers today are refreshed and released by the discovery that for several hundred years in Christian history there was considerable freedom and variety in the wording of the eucharistic prayer. They do not appear to feel the need to spell out in invariable words the precise meaning of the act. Similarly they are reassured by the fact that no one attempted to define such things as "the moment of consecration" or the precise mode of Christ's presence until centuries after Christians started making eucharist. Their response is not, it would seem, a mere shrug of impatience with doctrinal questions, nor a symptom of anti-intellectualism. Rather it appears to be a reaffirmation of the contextual character of worship, a recognition that the question, "What are we saying?" is a part of the larger question, "What are we doing?"

Secondly, the various Christian answers to the latter question have at least one thing in common. The major intention in celebrating the Lord's Supper appears always to have been obedience to the Lord's command, "Do this. . . ." Whatever additional interpretations and emphases have been made, agreement is complete that what Christians wanted to be doing was what the Lord wanted to have done.

The sixteenth century Reformers were convinced that the Lord's Supper was a normal part of worship on every Lord's Day. As Luther Reed has put it: "In rediscovering the Gospel, the Lutheran Reformation rediscovered the Sacrament." [14] The audible Word of Scripture demanded the complement of the Visible Word of the Sacrament. In the same spirit Calvin called the dissociation of Word from Sacrament "a vicious practice." He was unable to achieve weekly celebration in sixteenth century Geneva, but his concern for the Lord's command is clear: "We all confess then with one mouth that in receiving the sacrament in faith, according to the ordinance of the Lord, we are truly made partakers of the real substance of the body and blood of Jesus Christ. How this is done, some may deduce better and explain more clearly than others." [15] Influenced by the "New Divinity" from the Continent, Thomas Cranmer reflects the same intentional basis of the act when he tries to state for the Church of England "the true doctrine of the first catholic christian faith." Christ "hath prepared bread to be eaten and wine to be drunken of us in his holy supper. . . ." [16]

Thirdly, the eucharistic prayer in its fullness, according to the growing ecumenical consensus on the subject,[17] is intended to evoke and express thanksgiving to God the Father for the whole creation and for the whole history of redemption. It should therefore include special thanksgiving for the work of Christ, with an explicit *anamnesis* or memorial of his death and resurrection, as well as a recitation of the words which he is said to have used when he instituted the Supper. It should therefore include special thanksgiving for the work of the Holy Spirit in the Church, with an explicit *epiklesis* or invocation for his blessing upon the whole action of the worshipers, including their gifts of bread and wine.

The two terms *anamnesis* and *epiklesis* are of tremendous importance in the history of Christian worship. It is interesting to note a growing tendency in ecumenical documents to leave them untranslated, on the grounds that no other words can do justice to both their richness and their precision in the Greek. In very general terms, the Western Church has tended to stress anamnesis particularly of Christ's sacrifice on the cross, whereas the Eastern Church has tended to stress his resurrection and parousia. By the same token Roman Catholics and Anglicans have linked the essential act of consecration with the "institution narrative," whereas the Orthodox have tended to link the essential act with invocation of the Spirit. The contemporary theological mood resists such definitions.[18] God's act of coming to his people in worship, it is thought, cannot be tied to a verbal formula. What is most essential is to make eucharist, to give thanks for all the goodness of God.

The action which follows the eucharistic prayer is one which has far more importance in the meal than many modern worshipers have been taught to expect and to think about. The bread is broken. The New Testament tradition says it was in the breaking of bread that men recognized the presence of their Risen Lord. The act is intentionally linked with the Body of the Lord, broken before it could be shared. It recalls the unity of the participants in the One Body of which the worshipers are, and are about to receive, fragments.

It is not accidental that many contemporary liturgies recom-

mend that silence should be observed at the time of the fraction. This is, to be sure, one way to add dramatic emphasis to
this third action in the total meal. But more deeply, silence
is a testimony that this breaking of bread transcends man's
powers to express in words the reality he perceives. By keeping
silence, he is expressing the fragmentary character of his vision
as he contemplates and encounters the One who said: "This
is my body. . . ."

The restraint of all four New Testament versions of the
"eucharistic words of Jesus" points toward silence as essential
at and on this point. Some ancient manuscripts add "which is
given for you" to Luke's account of the words Jesus said when
he broke the bread and gave it to his disciples (Luke 22:19).
Other ancient manuscripts add "which is broken for you" to
Paul's account in I Cor. 11:24. But the best texts have the
fewest words. It is probably that the New Testament authors
were influenced by the tradition that the "mysteries" were only
disclosed to the faithful, so that one was therefore very careful in writing anything about them which might be read by
outsiders.[19] It is also probable that they were influenced by
silence *in* the "mysteries," in the liturgical act itself.

Whatever their differences of interpretation, Christian worshipers understand the eating and drinking which climax the
eucharistic meal with reference to the Body and Blood of
Christ, as effecting communion with him, and as effecting
communion with all members of the Body of Christ which is
the Church. There is a strong feeling on the part of many
Christians today, including those in the Roman Catholic and
Orthodox traditions, that communion should be the norm
rather than the exception for all present at the Eucharist.

The process by which in the Middle Ages communion became infrequent, and the sacrifice of the Mass divorced from
sacramental communion for the laity, has been investigated by
many able liturgical historians. One summary sketch sees
linguistic, architectural, and theological factors all contributing
to growing "sentiments of awe and fear" that kept people away
from communion.[20] Withholding the cup from the laity and

putting individual "hosts" directly into peoples' mouths instead of into their hands are seen as by-products of this exaggerated reverence.

From a phenomenological perspective it is clear that the loss of communal eating and drinking from the regular act of worship is also closely connected with overemphasis on "sacrifice" interpreted in terms of death. Rather than being reminded primarily of the bitterness of his death, worshipers, when the idea of Resurrection remained most central, were invited to communion with the song "Taste and see how sweet is the Lord." [21]

A "celebration" of the Lord's Supper, a Eucharist, is a festive occasion. Although Christians may "celebrate the Resurrection" (to use Cyprian's phrase for the whole service) in the morning, the meal is not an everyday breakfast. It is a feast. As such, it shares characteristics of feasts in general. When people prepare for a feast, they are always concerned with more than the food. Light and flowers, bright colors, special decorations and special clothing are part of festive behavior in all cultures. So are anticipation and jubilation.

Frédéric Debuyst, in a "little phenomenology of feast," has reported a study done by a psychology student at the University of Louvain. Children were shown three pictures and asked which of the three they would like for their own birthday feast. One picture showed a child standing in front of a table piled high with presents. A second showed a small family eating ice cream and cake together, with one large gift package beside the birthday child's place. The third picture showed no presents, just a large group of adults and children eating together around a table obviously decorated for a party. More than 70 per cent of the children studied are said to have chosen the third picture as the one they would like best for their own celebration. Their answers to the question "Why?" stressed the fact that the people were happy, that it was a "real" feast.[22]

In recent years Western Christians are stressing afresh elements of joy and thanksgiving and celebration in their worship meal. This current re-emphasis on the festive character of the Lord's Supper results in part from renewed awareness of biblical eschatology. It undoubtedly results also from greater contact between East and West in this ecumenical age.

The idea of an eschatological meal is prominent in such sayings of Jesus as "I tell you many will come from east and west and sit at table with Abraham, Isaac, and Jacob in the kingdom of heaven" (Mt. 8:11). It colors his many parables about banquets and wedding feasts. Luke's Gospel presents one of these as his direct response to a fellow-diner's remark: "Blessed is he who shall eat bread in the kingdom of God" (Lk. 14:14). Jesus drew explicitly on this popular thought of his day when he instituted the meal and commanded his disciples to continue it.

In all three synoptic accounts of the Last Supper, Jesus connects the Cup with drinking in the Kingdom. Luke's version of the saying is, "Take this, and divide it among yourselves; for I tell you that from now on I shall not drink of the fruit of the vine until the kingdom of God comes" (Lk. 22:17–18). Mark's version ends, "until that day when I drink it new in the kingdom of God" (14:25); and Matthew's adds "with you" to the saying (26:29). The Jerusalem Bible makes the eucharistic connection even more vivid by rendering the Matthean sentence, "From now on, I tell you I shall not drink wine until the day I drink the new wine with you in the kingdom of my Father."

Although the words of institution recited in the eucharistic prayers of the classic liturgies have sometimes combined the words over the Cup as they appear in I Cor. 11:24–25 with the words from Matthew 26:28, thus adding "which is poured out for many for the forgiveness of sins," they have not incorporated the next sentence, the one about drinking the new wine in the Kingdom. For in much Christian thought, the Eucharist *is* the Messianic banquet, and therefore the foretaste in the present of that feast of joy to which Jesus and his contemporaries looked forward.

Eastern liturgies have preserved this aspect of primitive Christian thought more vividly than Western rites, which have emphasized more the passion and death of the Lord. In describing the liturgy of the Eastern Orthodox Church, Ernst Benz, for example, begins with the Messianic banquet. The basic mood of the Church at the eucharistic meal, he says, is a mood of nuptial rejoicing. The creative core of the liturgy is the miracle "that in breaking bread with Christ in accordance with a ritual taught them by Jesus himself *at the Messianic wedding supper* the fellowship of the baptized are again in the presence of the Redeemer." [23]

At the conclusion of the Last Supper, according to strong suggestions in the Synoptic Gospels, the whole company sang together the 118th Psalm.[24] The song is part of the Hallel group which would have been used if the meal were a Paschal celebration. More importantly, it is a statement of praise for the victory which God brings out of suffering, for the salvation which he offers, for the triumph of life out of death. Toward the end of this eucharistic song occur the words which have been quoted not only in the New Testament when Jesus enters Jerusalem on the first "Palm Sunday" but also at thousands upon thousands of liturgical celebrations of the Eucharist: "Blessed is he who comes [or enters] in the name of the Lord" (Ps. 118:26).

The verse underlines both the festive character of the meal in which it is regularly used, and its eschatological dimension. The Lord who comes into the midst of the worshipers in a new way, as bread and wine are taken and blessed and broken and shared, is the Lord of whom Paul cries: "Christ our Passover is sacrificed; therefore let us keep the feast." This coming is, in some eucharistic thought, the Parousia for which the community prays.

Immediately after the line *Benedictus qui venit,* Psalm 118 (vv. 26b–27) continues in a significantly festal manner:

> We bless you from the house of the Lord, 5
>   The Lord is God
> and he has given us light.
> Bind the festal procession with branches,
>   up to the horns of the altar!

In place of "he has given us light," the Jerusalem Bible offers the translation, "he smiles on us."

Festival and celebration in biblical thought as in birthday parties demand, it seems, that experiences of tasting be associated with seeing, ideas of light associated with happiness. Celebration of the coming of the Lord accounts for the use in Christian worship of a cluster of visual symbols which only a deadly rationalism reduces to mere "visual aids." Rather, they prepare the celebrants (the people as a whole) for receiving him with gladsome mind. Candles, flowers, vestments; colored hangings and stained glass; frescoes and statues—a host of incidental accessories of worship generally recognized as adiaphora or nonessentials, deserve mention in this connection. We will limit our attention to two of these phenomena— the incense pot and the icon, and their roles in the Christian feast.

Young people today may be recovering some of the power of smell, if one can judge by their use of incense not only to mask the smell of marijuana, but also to evoke and express certain moods. Their discoveries have yet to effect a change in a deodorized generation or in Protestant tradition, however. Protestant worship has almost entirely dispensed with any appeal to the olfactory sense, except as it comes incidentally from the use of Christmas greens or Easter lilies.

The Reformers were influenced by prophetic denunciations of burnt offerings, no doubt, as a concomitant of rejecting what seemed to them to be exaggerated or false ideas of sacrifice in the Eucharist. Nevertheless, they did not reject the psalms which record so clearly the sensory interplay which is part of the worshiper's experience. If the Reformers were sure that Yahweh did not smell the pleasing fragrance of Noah's offerings, as Genesis claimed (8:21), they yet sang: "Let my prayer be set forth in thy sight as the incense; and let the lifting up of my hands be an evening sacrifice" (141:2). In other parts of the Church, incense has continued to be used, and to be explained with just such reference to smell and to sight.

The fragrance of the incense is more than appeal to smell, one apologist writes; "it denotes the offering of a sweet-smelling sacrifice to God." [25] Furthermore, he continues, the censer is "an image of the whole Body of Christ in space and time," to which the act of censing is intended to call attention.[26] He documents the latter point with an elaborately detailed allegorical symbolism in which the bowl of the censer, the lid, the chains, the attached bells, the coals, the fire and the smoke each stand for some part of the whole Church in heaven and in earth. The same idea is repeated in prayers chanted at the four sides of the altar as the elements of bread and wine are censed during the Syriac Liturgy. The Virgin Mary is remembered on the east; prophets, apostles, and martyrs, on the west; teachers and priests, the just and the righteous, on the north; the Church and all her children, on the south.[27]

Any attempt to translate a symbolic action into a series of concepts in this manner does a disservice to our embodied perception as the phenomenologist understands it. A living symbol communicates directly without requiring an intellectual intermediate step saying "this stands for that." But this account of censing nevertheless conveys notably the multisensory appeal of this act of worship. One smells the smoke, hears the bells, sees the fire (another of those ambivalent symbols in worship, since fire not only gives man light and warmth, but also burns him); and thereby, he sees the Church.

During the Divine Liturgy in Orthodox churches, the priest also censes the icons. Icons play an active role in Orthodox worship, but they cannot be understood apart from their liturgical context any more than can bread and wine. Hung in a frame on a wall, as an object of aesthetic interest, an icon ceases to be an icon, the Orthodox believe. "An icon divorced from a place and act of worship is a contradiction in terms." [28] Within that context, they serve the same function ascribed to the act of censing—they reveal or manifest the whole Church to the gaze and therefore to the persons who make common cause with their gaze. Like all art, they serve the purpose of alerting people to what they might have missed.

Three dimensions of Orthodox thought about icons deserve special mention. The first is that they are not three dimensional. Statues are expressly prohibited in Orthodox churches. As Leonid Ouspensky interprets the flat surface of the icon, "illusory three-dimensional space is replaced by the plane of reality." [29] It is considered a mirror or window surface, "a kind of window between the earthly and celestial worlds." [30] Since in Orthodox thought the mystery depicted in icons and the mystery enacted in the liturgy are one, both inwardly and outwardly, the icon thus repeats the theory that "within the sanctified space of the Church, heaven descends upon earth when the Eucharist is celebrated." [31] The words used in liturgical celebration on the Feast of Orthodoxy—the annual commemoration of the end of the iconoclastic struggle in the ninth century—declare that through the icons of Christ and of the Virgin, "we see in outline the tents of heaven, and we exult in holy joy." [32]

Icons are thus, first, a sacramental means of seeing heaven. They are, secondly, a sacramental means of seeing Man. St. John of Damascus, the great eighth century Orthodox theologian, gave classic expression to this central theme of the *imago* when he said (in his defense of holy icons) that the first great icon painter was "the Creator himself, God, the architect who decided to create the human being." [33] Man before the Fall was made in the image of God, the Bible says. The New Man, Christ, the Second Adam restores the image. He is "the image (ikon) of the invisible God, the first-born of all creation . . ." (Col. 1:15). Orthodox exposition of the meaning of icons thus puts great emphasis on the doctrines of the Incarnation and of the Transfiguration, as the beginning of the new creation of all men in Christ. In short, Jesus Christ is the perfect icon.

Icons are therefore, thirdly, a means of seeing the communion of saints, the whole Body of Christ, present and participant in every Eucharist. Iconologists say that no mere portrait of a saint could accomplish this, for icons are not visual aids but epiphanies of the saints in transfigured state.[34] A photograph, Paul Verghese puts it sharply, is a memento of someone who is absent; an icon indicates a presence.[35] Thus when the Orthodox are assembled at worship, the iconostasis before them presents Christ to the right of the "royal door" to the altar, and the Virgin Mary on the left. John the Baptist and the patron saint of the particular church have the second places to the right and left, respectively. On the door itself are the archangels Gabriel and Michael. Other icons have other traditional places assigned.

If icons are thus a means whereby the "inaugurated" eschatology of the Eucharist is made visible in the present space of worship, the iconostasis on which they appear may be a detriment to full apprehension of that future present. A screen between the worshipers and the altar is undoubtedly part cause and part effect of a decline in the Orthodox churches of regular communion through eating and drinking, comparable to that in Western Catholicism beginning in the Middle Ages.

At the end of the eucharistic prayer in the Divine Liturgy today, the Orthodox priest comes out through the door in the iconostasis holding high the chalice. A typical interpretation of the service written for laymen says: "The action of the priest coming out to the congregation with the holy cup signifies the Risen Christ bringing the food of eternal life to the faithful. Everyone *who wishes to receive communion* walks up to the altar at this point." [36] In most parishes, very few do so on ordinary Sundays. Vision has, it seems, overwhelmed tasting in the evolution of Orthodox response to the invitation "Taste and see the goodness of the Lord."

Such dangers of a visual narcosis in worship are one reason why we must consider in the next chapter the perennial iconoclastic movement in the Christian Church. By focusing in this one on the icon, a visual phenomenon more than slightly esoteric to most Western worshipers, however, we may have clouded an essential point. Before leaving the phenomena of tasting and seeing in Christian worship, therefore, we must insist more firmly upon the fact that seeing in worship has a profound relationship to all of man's seeing in the other spaces of his life.

Sight and insight are interdependent. Just such a recognition motivates contemporary concern for a liturgical art consonant with incarnational faith. Increasingly the "visual heresy" of bad art is taken seriously, precisely because what man sees with his eyes cannot be separated from what he believes in his heart and shows forth in his life.

The favorite images of modern Christians, Daniel Berrigan, S.J., has suggested, appear to canonize childhood and death. They stress the "childish, the comforting, the soft"; or they portray Christ undergoing an agonizing death. And, as he sees it, "bad art has a way of becoming bad theology. And bad theology in turn cripples life." [37] Such sentimental or defeated images foster a dream world which "can bear equally with injustice, poverty, segregation, the defacement of the image of Christ in the human family."

In contrast, the mosaics and frescoes which early Christian worshipers faced shaped a sense of reality. The great social scene they depicted of the whole company of saints in heaven and earth, was crowned by a figure of Christ—a Christ both adult and victorious. "He was Himself the Ikon, the exact and luminous Image, of what it means to be a man." [38]

The same point about what one sees and believes in worship is a major thesis of the Gospel according to St. John, according to Oscar Cullmann's study of early Christian worship.[39] Remembering in the Spirit, worshipers can with Thomas see in the Lord's hands the print of the nails, and respond: "My Lord and my God!" (John 20:28). Remembering in the Spirit, they can say with John: "We have seen his glory" (1:14).

Chapter 11

THE BREAKING OF IMAGES

SYMBOLS SLIP. All symbols slip. The symbol breakers who have appeared regularly in the Christian community, smashing other men's efforts to figure forth the One whom they worship, have recognized this. In this chapter we will look primarily at that Christian iconoclasm which manifests itself in prohibiting images and eating. But we will also listen to a new demand today for a more radical iconoclasm—one which calls into question all pretensions toward "purity" of worship.

The inescapable slipping of symbols has been catalogued astringently by Karl Jaspers. He identified five ways in which men continually allow such signs to become something else in their lives. Symbolism constantly degenerates, he claimed, into superstition, allegory, aestheticism, dogmatism, or magic.[1] All five of these mutations have appeared in Christian worship and have evoked iconoclastic reaction.

The first and last are most prominent in the earliest major iconoclastic movement in Christian history. Superstition results when the symbol is confused with empirical reality. Magic results when an effort is made to manipulate the symbol in order to achieve what man wants. Both magical and superstitious practices unquestionably came to be associated with the visual images of worship in the Eastern churches prior to the bitter iconoclastic struggle of the eighth century.

Among the milder instances which one historian of the period has reported is the popular belief that the bishop of Edessa saved that city from fire by carrying an image of Christ around its walls. Legend said that this image was one which Christ himself had sent to the King of Edessa. It was not an image painted by man, but one which the Lord created by pressing his own face against a piece of linen.[2] A comparable story had it that St. Luke painted an image of the Virgin, and that she herself had promised that her grace would accompany it wherever it went.

Christians did not wait seven hundred years before crying out against blatant popular misunderstanding of icons. The iconoclasts of the eighth century were able to gather abundant testimony from earlier Christian writers against the dangers of paganism. Even Clement of Alexandria, the Church Father perhaps most hospitable to a marriage between Athens and Jerusalem, could be quoted as denouncing pictorial art in the name of the Second Commandment. Early hostility to figural representation in the Christian cult is expressed most succinctly by a contemporary of Augustine who said: "When images are put up the customs of the pagans do the rest." [3]

Not until Leo III was crowned emperor in Constantinople in 717, however—indeed, not until he had been on the throne for some ten years—was there a major campaign, backed by the power of the state, to obliterate all such images from the spaces of Christian worship.

Under Leo's son, Constantine IV, a council of some 338 bishops announced, after deliberating for seven months, that "supported by the Holy Scriptures and the Fathers, we declare unanimously in the name of the Holy Trinity that there shall be rejected and removed and anathematised out of the Christian Church every likeness which is made out of any material and colour whatsoever by the evil art of painters." [4] It proclaimed also that the Emperor had saved the world from idolatry.

Neither the fascinating historical questions of the degree to which the surrounding Islamic iconoclasm influenced Constantine and his Council, nor the miserable details of how their decrees were subsequently enforced, need detain us here—although the latter are a stark reminder of the violence of human emotions about worship, and the depth of human resistance when cherished patterns are threatened. Rather we should note an apparent inconsistency in the practice of the iconoclasts, and the apparent literalism of their view of scripture.

When an image of Christ, condemned as "a lifeless, speechless, effigy of wood," was removed from the palace gates in Constantinople, it was replaced by a cross. Underneath this substitute symbol was inscribed a verse praising the imperial iconoclasts and concluding: "Thus what the Book forbids they did replace/With the believers' blessed sign of grace." [5]

Worship, the early iconoclasts seem to have argued, is man's response to the invisible, ineffable God. His law commands that man shall not make, bow down to, nor serve "any likeness of anything" in heaven or on earth. All images and all "bowing down" to them are therefore idolatrous. In exempting the sign of the cross from their sweeping condemnation, however, the iconoclasts were anticipating Paul Tillich's twentieth century claim that it is a unique symbol of faith, the one most immune by its nature to that slipping which besets all others.[6]

St. John of Damascus, arch-defender of images, was only the first of a long line of critics who raised the obvious question about this and other "blessed signs of grace": Why are pictures different from other material objects and symbols, including the Eucharist itself? [7] In the eighth century, at least as far as the surviving evidence goes, no one seems to have had an effective answer. The Damascene was also the first of a long line of Christian thinkers to call for sharper distinctions in what is meant by the word "worship."

His analysis of degrees of reverence led ultimately to the definition adopted by the Second Council of Nicea in 815, when the iconoclasts were overthrown. It distinguished between the "true worship" due only to the divine nature and the "honour" or "respect" paid to images. In English an equivalent contrast is frequently attempted by using "adoration" and "veneration" respectively to translate the Greek words used by the Council. That Council was also careful to relate other symbols to the symbols of the cross: ". . . just as the figure of the precious and life-giving Cross, so also the venerable and holy images, as well in painting and mosaic as of other fit materials, should be set forth in the holy churches of God. . . ." [8]

From a historical point of view there is very little connection to be found between the Byzantine iconoclastic controversies and the new iconoclasm which was part of the Reformation, but the phenomena are strikingly similar. Popular piety in fourteenth and fifteenth century Europe was marred by superstition and magic no less than that in eighth century Byzantium. In addition, allegory had become an elaborate intellectual game, whereby every activity of life was seen to have some contrived "religious meaning." Jaspers describes this third distortion of symbolism as a slipping into nonreality. John Calvin called it "child's play." [9]

In France and the Netherlands, as Huizinga has shown, "the need of adoring the ineffable in visible shapes was continually creating ever new figures." [10] Two examples will suffice. Devout Christians began to keep little statues of the Virgin which opened up to show the Trinity inside.[11] At the conclusion of their sermons, Franciscan preachers would hold up a blue-painted board bearing the name "Jesus" in golden letters encircled by a sunburst. A contemporary observer reports that "the people filling the church kneel down and weep with emotion." [12]

The sense of sight, it seems, overwhelmed all others in the twilight of the Middle Ages. Such extravagant visual symbols help one to understand John Calvin's insistence that faith comes by hearing. The Reformers denounced idolatry in worship by appealing to Scripture with even greater consistency than the earlier iconoclasts. Calvin's commentary on the Pentateuch, which may be taken as representative, puts all Old Testament regulations for worship under the heading of the

Second Commandment, which he called "a remedy to all external and manifest superstitions." [13] He rejects outright the argument, a favorite in the West from the time of Gregory the Great, that images serve as "the books of the unlearned." [14] God, Calvin says, is "insulted when He is clothed in a corporeal image . . . the object of Moses is to restrain the rashness of men, lest they should travesty God's glory by their imaginations." [15] Hence the commandment against graven images is applied explicitly to statues and pictures by which "the spiritual worship of God is corrupted."

With his usual intellectual clarity, Calvin sees the weakness in some arguments which were being used by less dispassionate iconoclasts. After all, Isaiah "saw the Lord," and Ezekiel, his vision—although that was one, Calvin observes, that no painter could represent.[16] One cannot argue from Scripture, therefore, that it is always enough to hear God's voice. Nevertheless he sees greater weakness in that customary "trifling distinction" between real worship and mere honor.[17] To Calvin's mind, the term "idolatry" includes all corrupt worship. The Law forbids *all* forms and ceremonies which involve wood and stone. God's purpose was to raise men's minds, not to keep them earthbound; whereas the idolaters want to draw God down to themselves. Whatever "holds down and confines our senses to the earth, is contrary to the covenant of God." [18] John Calvin had not read Merleau-Ponty.

Anglican church leaders under Elizabeth I, however, had read and thoroughly digested their Calvin. In 1563 the ministers of the Church of England were charged to read aloud in worship services the wholesome doctrine of the Second Book of Homilies. One of these homilies was "Against the Perils of Idolatry." The iconoclastic doctrine in it goes far beyond Calvin's. It calls upon bishops or civil magistrates not only to remove from the churches but to destroy all pictures and statues with any religious significance whatsoever.[19] Puritan leaders of the seventeenth century who did precisely that were doing something still enjoined by the official documents of the Church of England which they had repudiated.

Reaction against such visual austerity is strong in our own century. Even before the First World War, a Protestant theologian is heard lamenting the fact that through Calvin orthodox Protestants have inherited a tendency to construe the Word rather than to represent it. In *Christ on Parnassus,* his lectures on art, ethics, and theology, P. T. Forsyth argues eloquently that in killing idolatry, the Second Commandment killed plastic imagination. Yet he tries to appreciate the iconoclastic drive. "There is something incomplete in artistic taste," he believes, "until it sees . . . the beauty of Puritanism. . . . There is not much beauty in mere insensibility to beauty but there may be very much in its renunciation." [20]

In terms of Jasper's critique introduced at the beginning of this chapter, one detects here the danger of a slipping of symbols into an attitude of aesthetic detachment. A similar aestheticism seems to be a major criterion in current Christian writing both for and against the use of visual images in the spaces of worship today.

One modern Calvinist, for example, recognizes that there can be subtle false gods of the ear as well as of the eye.[21] To refute those who say that the Image of God disappeared from sight on Ascension Day, leaving us only with words, he uses essentially the same incarnational argument developed by John of Damascus in behalf of the eighth century iconophiles. An image of absence, he points out, does not conform to the Incarnation.[22] Formlessness is itself a manner of form. The essential question is *what* signs and images will be used in worship. The Second Commandment does not prohibit all images, just false ones. Good images safeguard the imagination.

At a time when a Protestant monk is cautiously reappraising images, however, the Bishops of the Roman Church are counseling a modified form of iconoclasm. The pronouncement of the Vatican Council calls for noble beauty rather than sumptuous display in sacred art, and for removing from churches works which lack artistic worth.[23] Although one commentator notes, regretfully, that "it cannot be expected that our bishops will go round our churches in an iconoclastic fury sweeping away all this pretentious and fundamentally irreligious farrago," [24] another suggests that the absence of superfluous images is itself an image of the invisible God of whom the Bible speaks. [25]

Renunciation of tasting has a place in Christian worship as prominent and as ambiguous as that renunciation of seeing which culminates in vehement destruction of images. Not eating and not drinking are also powerful symbols in man's experience and hence in his religions. Men who hunger and thirst associate their physical discomfort with their other unfilled needs and desires; they link their craving for bodily nourishment with all their cravings for good things. In this sense, the two versions of Jesus' saying on the subject are complementary: The Matthean "spiritualized" beatitude, "Blessed are those who hunger and thirst for righteousness, for they shall be satisfied" (Mt. 5:6), has its necessary roots in the ungarnished Lukan form, "Blessed are you that hunger now. . . . Woe to you that are full now . . ." (Lk. 6:21, 25).

Fasting, deliberately going without food and drink for religious purposes, appears to express two major intentions, both of them reflected in appearances of the practice from the first to the twentieth centuries. It bespeaks community sorrow. It enables personal closeness to God and to fellow men.

A fast is, of course, the antithesis of a feast. The early Christians were evidently hyperconscious of this dimension of meaning—so much so that it was a source of some controversy. All of the Synoptics report the question as posed to Jesus, why don't your disciples fast? His answer is said to have been: "Can the wedding guests fast while the bridegroom is with them? As long as they have the bridegroom with them they cannot fast. The days will come, when the bridegroom is taken away from them, and they will fast in that day" (Mk. 2:19–20).

Guided by this logic, the Church expressly forbade fasting on the day of eucharistic feast. A fourth century council even passed a law decreeing: "If any one, under pretense of asceticism, shall fast on Sunday, let him be anathema." [26] By the same logic, the Church appears to have had for a long time only two general and as it were official fast days, the Friday and Saturday before Easter—the days as Tertullian notes, in which "the Bridegroom is taken away." [27] A similar limitation to two days of general fast still appears in the Book of Common Prayer, although the two in question have become Ash Wednesday and Good Friday.

In contrast with the communal nature of festivals, most fasting, therefore, is regarded by the Church as essentially a private and individual matter. The injunction in Matthew 6:16, "when you fast, do not look dismal . . ." is intended to make sure that a fast may not be obvious to other men; but the "when" seems to presuppose that individual Christians will continue this religious practice along with prayer and almsgiving, the trilogy of devotional disciplines inherited from Judaism.

Even after he became a member of the rigorist Montanist sect, Tertullian spoke of fasting "according to the times and needs of each individual." [28] The traveler Etheria noted with great interest how varied were individual times and needs in Jerusalem in the mid-fourth century. After reporting that Lenten fasts ranged from eating only once a week after service on the Lord's Day, through eating only one meal each day, she added: "For no one exacts from any how much he should do, but each does what he can, nor is he praised who has done much, nor is he blamed who has done less; that is the custom here." [29] Etheria also observed in Jerusalem a custom already ancient in her day, that of fasting every Wednesday and Friday throughout the year. This Christian variation on the prior Jewish practice of fasting two days each week was known in Rome before the end of the New Testament period.[30]

The fasting Christian evidently identifies himself with the general intent of Jesus' quotation from Deuteronomy: "Man shall not live by bread alone. . . ." The full dimensions of such a saying are beyond measure. In a marvelously iconoclastic fashion, it challenges the very heart of Christian worship, as Dostoevski recognized when he had the Great Inquisitor rebuke Jesus for resisting the temptation to turn stones into bread during his fast in the wilderness: "Choosing bread, Thou wouldst have satisfied the universal and everlasting craving of humanity—to find someone to worship . . . to worship what is beyond dispute." [31] By not eating one's daily bread, one acknowledges the limitations even of his taste of the "Bread of Heaven" in the Eucharist.

Beyond this, there is a manifest two-directional pull in the understanding of those who choose to fast. To oversimplify, it is interpreted with reference to serving God and to serving the neighbor. Fasting thus relates both to prayer and to almsgiving. The former note is struck in the now archaic-sounding words of the Book of Common Prayer listing "other days of fasting on which the Church requires such a measure of abstinence as is more especially suited to extraordinary acts and exercises of devotion." The latter note is sounded in language of the same era by the poet Robert Herrick:

> Is it to quit the dish
>   Of Flesh, yet still
>   To fill
> The platter high with Fish?
>   . . .
> No: 'tis a Fast, to dole
>   Thy sheaf of wheat,
>   And meat,
> Unto a hungry Soule.[32]

In pursuit of the first intentional pole, such Christian worshipers as the Desert Fathers and some of the medieval mystics have been led to extremes of fasting which their moderate brethren deplore. But there is widespread human testimony that the really hungry man has extraordinary experiences. Reports of heightened perception, even with auditory and visual concomitants, cannot be lightly dismissed as "mere hallucination." In obedience to the second intentional pole, such

Christian worshipers as St. Francis and George Fox went often hungry so that other men might eat.

In our day the enacted symbolism of fasting appears to have slipped almost out of the ken of many well-fed Christians, to be discovered anew by secular youth with precisely the same twofold intention. Many people under thirty express their hunger for encounter with reality by embracing both the meditational disciplines of the East and the kind of restricted diet which makes that meditation effective. A student reporting on a five-day fast in a campus sorority house expresses clearly the other dimension: "Not surprisingly the act of fasting itself makes one conscious of things she may have previously not been thinking about or concerned with. . . . After you fast for several days, you get tired and rundown, your mind gets boggled, you begin to realize what it is like to be less intelligent than you are; you also begin to understand the plight of a poor grape-worker, a Mississippi cotton worker, or a starving Biafran." [33]

Religious symbols appear to have retained more cultural relevance than many prophets of secularism allow. Yet this kind of not-eating can be taken as a splendid example of what Gabriel Vahanian has called a false iconoclasm, a modern Promethean substitute for the authentic biblical iconoclasm which he believes to be an essential feature of Christian faith. The new versions may seem radically iconoclastic, Vahanian says, but they are basically efforts at self-deification or forms of ethnolotry. They share the same self-deluding perfectionism which was evident in the extremes of Byzantine and Puritan picture-breaking. True iconoclasm is equally opposed to "this-worldly" and to "other-worldly" perfectionisms.

Vahanian's concept of authentic iconoclasm challenges not only religious man's efforts to hoard God's manna (against which the Christian tradition of fasting is a constant witness), but the whole tradition of liturgical worship which we have been describing in these pages. He calls on Christianity to smash its own golden calf.

Faith is impossible without culture, Vahanian recognizes;

it must incarnate itself in forms, institutions, and rites. But by these, it is betrayed.[34] God cannot be held captive. As soon as it ceases to be iconoclastic, religion degenerates. The present degeneration of the Christian tradition, as he sees it, results from a loss of iconoclastic nerve.[35] Radical opposition to man's tendencies to divinize his symbolic events and institutions is a *sine qua non* of biblical faith. Without constant protest in the manner of the prophets, images intended as windows and mirrors become opaque screens, obstacles between man and the living God he worships.[36] That God is imageless. It takes "iconoclastic audacity" to believe in him.[37]

In *Wait Without Idols,* Vahanian develops the thesis that Christianity has forfeited to literature its iconoclastic responsibility. The book takes its title from a question posed by W. H. Auden: "How can he wait without idols to worship . . . ?"[38] The same question in different words appears on all sides today. A contemporary theologian asks: "Does the 'death of God' mean the death of religious word and sign?"[39] A modern mystic who also sees symbols as idols calls also for iconoclastic waiting: "God and the supernatural are hidden and formless in the universe. . . . Christianity (Catholic and Protestant) speaks too much about holy things."[40] A modern composer explores in operatic form "the ultimately tragic gap between what is apprehended and that which can be said." As Aaron exults in imagining God, Moses cries out: "No image can give you an image of the unimaginable."[41]

Christian worship, as we said at the outset, is the heir of Jewish worship. As such, it is forever indebted both to Aaron and to Moses, both to priest and to prophet. In the creeds some Christians recite in worship, they acknowledge ever anew that God spoke by the prophets. That confession of faith commits worshipers to hear the word of the Lord when he said: "I hate, I despise your feasts, and I take no delight in your solemn assemblies. . . . Take away from me the noise of your songs. . . . But let justice roll down like waters, and righteousness like an ever-flowing stream" (Amos 5:21–24).

Christian worship, as we also said at the outset, is equally the result of a new commandment, the response to a new event. As such, it is worship in the name of one who took the form of a servant, the servant of whom it was said, "he had no form or comeliness." The really radical iconoclasm of Christian faith appears to be that which calls the worshipers not just to wait without idols, but to walk in love.

That breaking of images which is truly central in Christian worship, therefore, is the very Breaking of the Bread. In this action, worshipers are invited regularly to perceive that incarnation is itself iconoclastic.[42]

The liturgy as a whole, the full public act of worship, continually reflects the Christian experience of seeing-and-not-seeing. It is the symbolic and embodied corollary of faith and hope. When the meaning of the act is thought to be fully comprehended, then indeed the liturgy has turned to stone. Then, indeed, its symbolism has slipped into the fifth and last of the pitfalls Jaspers identified—into dogmatism. Consolidated meanings can become idols.[43] Liturgical idolatry appears inevitable when worshipers forget St. Paul's insight that "now we are seeing a dim reflection in a mirror."

Chapter 12

WORSHIP AND ACTION

AT THE END of the Service of the Word and the Lord's Supper each week, the assembly is dismissed. This final event in the action each Lord's Day sends the worshipers out into the spaces of their ordinary lives, back into the times of their workaday world with a renewed responsibility. The fact that the whole service took one of its names from the Latin words of dismissal spoken at that boundary line is fitting testimony to the importance it has in understanding the whole phenomenon.

Those who think about the end of the service today are conscious of the extent to which it summarizes what has been happening. Accordingly they are agreed that medieval tendencies to blur the boundary line were unfortunate. Multiplied devotions public and private at the conclusion of the liturgy, obscure the essential tone of this final statement. This moment, like so many others in the whole sequence, would appear to be one with two dimensions. It reminds worshipers of both the Godward and the manward thrust of what they have been doing.

The former pole leads some to stress a "blessing" at this point. Although they believe that God's blessing has been abundantly bestowed through the Word and the Sacrament, they think it is appropriate to conclude with a summary declaration of that blessing. The whole of worship is under-

171

stood as response to God's initiative, a thankful acknowledgment of his Coming into the midst of his people. As they leave the meeting, they would depart in the Peace which he gives.

Because they share this understanding of what has been happening, other Christians today prefer to stress at this moment the responsibility with which they are therefore charged. To participate in the liturgy which is the public work of worship is to accept a commission. From the service just ended, they are sent forth to serve. This mission is expressed in the final words now being used, in this or a similar form, in many Protestant churches: "Go out into the world in peace. Be strong and of good courage. Hold fast what is good. Love and serve the Lord, rejoicing in the power of the Holy Spirit."

The liturgical renewal in the churches has brought with it, that is, deepened awareness of the daily work of all the people of God, a work which is the direct concern of worship. In the New Testament, "liturgy" was understood as the total response of the Body of Christ. Obedience and service were not isolated from worship. Almost without exception, those today who write about the meaning of Christian worship insist on this essential connection.[1] Active worship promotes social change.

Their point is not that individuals hear moral imperatives in church and rush out to do "good works." Rather, it is thought, the community experiences in worship the social reality which it is charged to show forth, to embody in the world.

In his recent book aptly titled *The Worldliness of Worship*, James F. White of Southern Methodist University develops this thesis forcibly. He sees worship as "a model of the world." It is an activity in which both God and men participate, and one in which man thereby recognizes the true nature of his life. "God gives His work to man and man performs his work as an offering to God."[2] As a consequence, worship "expands the frontiers of our lives."[3] Men learn through worship that to be God's people in the world means to be servants of the one body of mankind.

Virtually the same understanding led the British Roman Catholic Brian Wicker to call the liturgical assembly "the paradigm of all human society." [4] In encounter with Christ through the communal action of the liturgy men experience relationships that are the norm for all social life. It generates the motives for action to transform society.

The social consequences of worship are similarly stressed when worship is defined as "acknowledgment of responsible dependency." [5] Through such acknowledgment man is freed from his "awful autonomy," and freed for being in community. Worship, the deliberate act of acknowledging such dependency and such responsibility, is seen as both awakening and sustaining responsible personhood. Or again, when worship is given an eschatological orientation, a like manward thrust is discovered. After experiencing a foretaste of that which is to come, one realizes more sharply that it is not yet here. The community recognizes, therefore, that it "ought not to stand, like the Apostles, gazing up at the cloud into which Christ has vanished and in which he will come again; but that our task is to go out to meet the world and bear visible witness there of Christian holiness." [6]

Although in different accents, all four of these voices speak from a common conviction that Christian worship is the antithesis of an escape from reality. It is not something to do after you get your pajamas on and are all ready to go to sleep, as many children are led to believe. It is the Christians' response to Easter morning. Rejoicing in the new day, rejoicing in the power of the Holy Spirit, they say Amen! at the end of their worship, and go out to "love and serve the Lord."

At the end of this study of the Service of the Word and the Lord's Supper, therefore, we can draw from the phenomena we have been looking at and listening to, some conclusions about the nature of Christian worship, and raise again some of the questions we started with. Choice and change, tension and ambiguity, form and freedom are inherent in the action which Christians believe—using time-space imagery from the prophet Malachi—is appropriate from sunrise to sunset and from East to West. Which is to say, always and everywhere.

First, to worship as a Christian is to choose a stance toward life, one way of being in the world, and deliberately to practice, to exercise that posture. In the pluralistic, secularized society of which he is a part, no Christian today is able to worship simply because it is the socially accepted thing to do. If he chooses to order his time and his space around the time and place of his assembling with others to meet the Lord, he is no longer in danger of being approved as a "nice person"; he is increasingly recognized as a nonconformist.

He is thus approaching a minority position more nearly that of his Christian brethren in the third century. Yet he is not choosing to live in the past. He is electing to move forward in memory and hope toward the future he believes God will bring. He uses the rear view mirror, as it were, to keep him surely oriented toward the One who is to Come. Furthermore, he has chosen Easter as how "time comes to life." [7] He finds in weekly celebration of that Easter event a dynamic for all his weeks and years; and in the place of that celebration, a shape for all his communities.

In choosing this activity, secondly, Christians are opening themselves to change. They ask that their ears be opened that they may hear the Word in the words. They look for their eyes to be opened that they may recognize the Risen Lord in the breaking of the bread. They expect to move and be moved, to touch and be touched. And this ritual action they interpret as a means of learning how to grow up in love. They would learn to feel this programme not only in the brain, but in the bone and pulse. [8] They seek to be themselves reshaped, re-created, conformed to another image. In taking seriously the symbolic and iconic character of their worship, they are aware that through the imaginations of men's hearts men's lives are shaped.

It follows, thirdly, that worship conceived as a time in which something is expected to happen, as an occasion for change, will be experienced as a time of tension. A function of Christian worship is to disturb the worshipers. To energize them for action. To strengthen them for service. Because the word "comfort" has lost this old strong meaning, it now contributes a false idea of what Christian worship is intended to do. Where the Word of God is truly preached and the Sacraments duly administered, Christians are summoned to wake from sleep.

Two Christian ideas which appear greatly to heighten appropriate tension and to preclude somnambulism are those of the Second Coming of Christ and of Heaven. Renewed affirmation of the Second Coming in worship has recently been singled out as a prime example of a credibility gap causing grave disaffection with the Church.[9] One might respond in the words of Northrop Frye that the literal-minded are imaginative illiterates.[10] Frye sees art as "a dream for awakened minds."[11] The same description can well be applied to the Christian liturgy.

When eschatological images, either the temporal one of a new Advent or the spatial one of Heaven, are used in worship, they help both to evoke and to express the gap between the already of Christ's presence in worship and the not-yet of his glory manifest to all mankind. Only to mundane literalists do they say go climb a tree to await his coming, or endure patiently until you are removed to some other place. In the enacted hope of worship, they say go forth to serve in love, and in confidence that his End will be victorious.

An atrophy of the religious imagination always increases the danger of literalism. Literalism in turn hardens, as we have seen, into idolatry—idolatry which can manifest itself as much toward the words of worship as toward its other symbols. All symbols, including symbolic actions, appear to serve most powerfully in worship when they remain ambiguous. The whole person must then be actively engaged in the work of perception and encounter. The meaning of his action is accessible neither through abstract concepts, nor through static definitions.

Iconoclastic movements in worship testify regularly against idolizing sounds and sights; but, as we have discovered, iconoclasm can itself become hardened into an idolatrous literalism. Silence, because it is essentially indeterminate, is a potent instrument in worship; but it, too, involves risk. It can speak loudly of not caring. So also with other forms of "formlessness." The refusal to allow images can be seen as an image of the invisible God; it can also be seen as an image of his absence.

The risks inherent in worship appear to be the risks inherent in being human—the risks of confusing the creature with the creator, the finite with the infinite, oneself with ultimate reality. In the central Christian tradition of worship, however, there is an acceptance of that risk. The Christian community has affirmed its own embodied nature in worship, because it has there affirmed its faith that the Man whom men killed, God has raised up again.

In its evolved form, Christian worship appears to have a duality which is analogous to the Christological doctrine of two natures in One Person. It is tempting to see in the history of liturgy, problems parallel to the difficulties Christians have had in thinking "without confusion and without separation" about the One through whom they worship. Such reflections lie outside the descriptive task we have undertaken, however.

What we have been chiefly describing is a single yet complex community action, a public work of worship which in its fullness contains freedom-in-form. It includes elements both of taking a stand, and of standing outside the normal times and places of experience so that they may be heard and seen anew. Some elements in the form appear to be akin to ordered games, or to a purposeful March. Other elements appear to be affiliated with sheer frolic, or with an unpredictable Happening. Both dimensions are essential. As Christians worship in response to the death and resurrection of Jesus Christ, so that response is a dance both grave and gay. As they interpret the meaning of what they are doing, many of them could sum it up in the words of Snoopy: "To dance is to live."

In the introduction, I cited four reasons for attempting another study of Christian worship. Each of them appeared to pose questions for today's worshipers. Finally, I pose in the form of summary theses four parallel convictions emerging from the foregoing pages. The materials we have been reviewing do not provide final answers to these questions, as should be self-evident; but they do seem to me to offer direction for thinking about the current problems confronting worship.

1. Christian worship is most alive when it is most fully embodied. The phenomenological understanding of perception, for which Merleau-Ponty has been our chief spokesman, appears to be thoroughly consistent with the fact that Christianity (and so, too, its worship) is not concerned with the immortality of the soul but with resurrection of the body. The understanding of cultural dynamism as dependent on a harmonious interplay among all the senses, for which Marshall McLuhan argues, appears to be thoroughly illustrated in the lively worship of the early Christian centuries. "Mind" and "heart" and "soul" are actively engaged, it seems, when man uses his ears and his eyes, his hands and his feet—and even his nose—in the work of worship. The call for incarnate love which Norman O. Brown has issued comes to those who worship in the name of an Incarnate Lord as a call freely to acknowledge and express their own creaturehood.

2. Christian worship is most itself when it is most consciously eschatological. The claim of the past on the present is therefore also the claim of the future on the present. If the norm of Christian worship be found in the Scripture and Tradition to which the Christian community gives authority, then it will always include in some form the prayer "Thy Kingdom come!" Liturgical historians have helped Christians to rediscover the relationship between active participation of the people of God in worship, and genuine expectation of God's coming into their midst. A dialectic of memory and hope gives dynamism to Christian worship. Given the method adopted in this book, a theological fuzziness about the Last Things of eschatology has been both deliberate and inevitable. Worshipers need help from theologians in thinking more about these matters. Yet the practical consequences seem to be enormous. Because the reign of God is a future which confronts Christians as present in worship, encounter with that future provides the imperative for changing the present.[12]

3. Worship in the ecumenical age should seek to make special room for the witness of Christian silence, and for the outpouring of the Spirit. The threat which individual worshipers feel when their accustomed patterns of worship are challenged appears to be in part appropriate and inescapable, because worship, as we have seen, is a way in which the believer discovers, expresses, and continually renews his grasp on reality. When that hold is shaken, he feels the earth quake. But this, according to the language of the New Testament, is precisely what Christians who remember in the Spirit the death and resurrection of Jesus Christ should expect to have happen.[13] And this, according to one keen observer, is what young people today want to have happen; they seek in worship as elsewhere "an electric circus of the spirit." [14] Forgetting the need to distinguish among spirits, some Christians fear all enthusiasm. It is possible, in that manner, as St. Paul warned, to quench the Spirit.[15]

4. Tomorrow's world is what Christian worship is about. Its essential elements as we have described them are to a remarkable degree parallel with those characteristics which contemporary film critics are discovering in the art of motion pictures. One could almost answer our major question—what is worship?—by directly paraphrasing their understanding of cinema. Worship is indeed an environment that you put on. It, too, offers a time-space environment in which beautiful things happen. It, too, celebrates change. The worshiper, even more than the film viewer, makes a commitment and invests himself in the action.[16]

Unlike the sights and sounds of films, however, the sights and sounds, the motions and emotions of Christian worship, open up a new world not of man's dreaming. The symbols of Christian worship cannot be invented; they are given. Contemporary liturgists know well that artificial symbols are not symbols, but traps.[17] The work facing Christian worshipers as they respond to the new world is not to contrive a new symbolic language, but to learn with expectation and gladness the full vocabulary of making eucharist.

Author's Notes

Introduction

1. For lack of a synonym for the German *Religionswissenschaft,* the cumbersome "history of religions" has come to be used. The literal "science of religions" will not do, nor the still popular "comparative religions" which presupposes some known standard of comparison. The English language needs a new term.

2. *Phenomenology of Perception* (Routledge and Kegan Paul, 1962), p. viii. Most of this Preface has been reprinted as "What is Phenomenology?", pp. 356–374 in Joseph Kockelmans, ed., *Phenomenology: The Philosophy of Edmund Husserl and Its Interpretation* (Doubleday Anchor Book, 1967), which is a useful introduction to the whole movement. For a more extensive survey see Herbert Spiegelberg, *The Phenomenological Movement: A Historical Introduction* (Martin Nijhoff, 19(J), 2 vols.

3. Quoted by Gerardus van der Leeuw in *Religion in Essence and Manifestation: A Study in Phenomenology,* Vol. II (Harper Torchbook, 1963). See Chapter 110 for his "History of Phenomenological Research."

Chapter 1: At All Times

1. *E.g., Myths, Dreams, and Mysteries* (Harper Torchbook, 1967), pp. 24, 30. *Cf. The Sacred and the Profane* (Harcourt, Brace, & Co., 1959), pp. 68–113. For other interpretations of Eliade see John Knox, *Myth and Truth* (The University Press of Virginia, 1964); Kenneth Hamilton, "*Homo Religiosus* and Historical Faith," *Journal of Bible and Religion* XXXIII (July, 1965), 213–222; and especially the assessment of Thomas J.J. Altizer, *Mircea Eliade and the Dialectic of the Sacred* (Westminster Press, 1963), which reaches conclusions opposing those here set forth.

2. *Myth and Reality* (Harper & Row, 1963), p. 19. See W. Taylor Stevenson's summary of this work in his stimulating *History as Myth* (Seabury Press, 1969), pp. 16 ff.

3. *The Myth of Eternal Return* (Pantheon Books, 1954), p. 89.

4. *Myth and Reality*, p. 169.

5. *Myths, Dreams, and Mysteries*, p. 30.

6. *Ibid.* It should be noted in support of Eliade's thesis that public readings of passages from the Old Testament, the Acts of the Apostles, and the Apocalypse in the context of Roman Catholic worship may still be announced by the words "In illo tempore. . . ." *Cf.* A. Croegaert, *The Mass of the Catechumens* (Cardinal Books, 1963), p. 197.

7. *Myth and Reality*, p. 169.

8. *Ibid.*

9. See, *e.g.*, the Commentary in *An Order of Worship* recommended by the Consultation on Church Union (Forward Movement Publications, 1968), pp. 39 ff.; and Eugene R. Fairweather, "Worship and the Sacraments: Some Ecumenical Trends," *Religion in Life* XXXII (Spring, 1963), 201–211.

10. *Cf.* Louis Bouyer, "Jewish and Christian Liturgies," *Cross Currents* XIII (Summer, 1963), 335–348.

11. For a summary see Josef A. Jungmann, *The Early Liturgy* (University of Notre Dame Press, 1959), pp. 29–38. *Cf.* also Massey H. Shepherd, Jr., "The Origin of the Church's Liturgy", Ch. 5 in the volume he edited, *Worship in Scripture and Tradition* (Oxford University Press, 1963).

12. "The Meaning of the Mass," *Modern Catholic Thinkers* (Harper & Row, 1960; A. Robert Caponigri, ed.), p. 280.

13. See, *e.g.*, Massey H. Shepherd, Jr., *Liturgy and Education* (The Seabury Press, 1965), pp. 40 ff. where current discussion of Hebrews is cited in the chapter on "The Christian Abolition of the Cult."

14. See Henry Bettenson, ed., *Documents of the Christian Church* (Oxford University Press, 1947), p. 6.

15. For the complicated story of this document see Jungmann, *The Early Liturgy*, pp. 52–58. Major portions of the text are available in paperback in Paul F. Palmer, ed., *Sacraments and Worship* (Sources of Christian Theology, Vol. I; Darton, Longman & Todd, 1957), and in Bard Thompson, *Liturgies of the Western Church* (Meridian Books, 1962).

16. *The Philosophy of Symbolic Forms* II (Yale University Press, 1955), 119.

17. *Didache* x; Palmer, *op. cit.*, p. 3.

18. *Christ the Sacrament of Encounter with God* (Sheed and Ward, 1963), p. 41.

Chapter 2: Motion and Emotion

1. See especially Ch. I, 14. J. D. Crichton, *The Church's Worship: Considerations on the Liturgical Constitution of the Second Vatican Council* (Geoffrey Chapman, 1965) includes the official text translated by Clifford Howell, S. J. Crichton comments that the liturgy is "in the order of *action* and until it reaches that order it does not exist," p. 100.

2. An "Open Letter" addressed to the Third German Liturgical Congress, meeting in Mainz in April, 1964; reprinted in *Herder Correspondence* (Special Issue, 1964), pp. 24–26.

3. J.-J. von Allmen, *Worship: Its Theology and Practice* (Oxford, 1965), p. 193.

4. Richard Paquier, *Dynamics of Worship* (Fortress Press, 1967; Donald Macleod, tr.).

5. See Alan Watts, *Beyond Theology* (Pantheon Books, 1964), p. 32.

6. *The Burning Fountain* (Indiana University Press, 1954), Ch. 9, "The Semantics of Ritual." This chapter has been omitted from the revised paperback edition of 1968.

7. *Phenomenology of Perception* (Routledge and Kegan Paul, 1962; Colin Smith, tr.), p. xi.

8. *Ibid.,* p. 124.

9. *Ibid.,* pp. 112 ff.

10. Joseph A. Kockelmans, "Merleau-Ponty's Phenomenology of Language," *The Review of Existential Psychology and Psychiatry* III (1963), 70.

11. (Beacon Press, 1967; 1st French ed., 1942), p. 188.

12. Roger W. Westcott, "Introducing Coenetics: A Biosocial Analysis of Communication," *The American Scholar* 35 (1966), 350.

13. *Op. cit.,* pp. 124 ff.

14. *Phenomenology of Perception,* p. 144.

15. *Ibid.,* p. 178.

16. *Ibid.,* p. 267.

17. *The Structure of Behavior,* p. 180.

18. *Mircea Eliade and the Dialectic of the Sacred,* p. 175. See his discussion pp. 176–200 for Nietzsche's later development of the theme of Dionysus as it relates to Eliade.

19. Friedrich Nietzsche, *The Birth of Tragedy and the Case of Wagner* (Vintage Books, 1967; Walter Kaufmann, tr.), p. 46.

20. *Ibid.,* p. 72.

21. *Ibid.,* p. 46.

22. Walter Kaufmann, *ibid.,* p. 4. Gerald Larson has recently suggested that as a young man Nietzsche spent many evenings at the home of J. J. Bachofen, who distinguished between Dionysian and Apollonian religion in his pioneer work on "Myth, Religion and

Mother Right," *Union Seminary Quarterly Review* XXIII (1968), 298.

23. *Ibid.,* p. 81. Kaufmann argues for the spelling Apollinian; but elsewhere I have followed the more general use.

24. *Ibid.,* p. 75.

25. Gerhard Delling, *Worship in the New Testament* (The Westminster Press, 1962; Percy Scott, tr.), p. 39. See also his Appendix, "On Dionysian Ecstasy," and *cf.* Walter F. Otto, *Dionysus: Myth and Cult* (Indiana University Press, 1965; Robert B. Palmer, tr.).

26. *Cf., e.g.,* Acts 2:13; II Cor. 12:2 ff.; Rev. 1:10.

27. *The Mind and Heart of Love* (Meridian Books, 1956), p. 271.

28. *Ibid.,* p. 223.

29. *Ibid.,* p. 275.

30. (Holt, Rinehart and Winston, 1963), p. 35.

31. Ernst Benz, *The Eastern Orthodox Church* (Aldine Publishing Co., 1963), p. 24.

32. *Cf.* Lawrence Fellows, "Revolution Transforms Christianity in Black Africa," *The New York Times,* Dec. 25, 1967.

33. Quoted from S. S. Greenslade, *Schism in the Early Church* (S.C.M. Press, 1953), p. 91.

34. *Op. cit.,* p. 39.

35. *Ibid.,* p. 60.

36. *Ibid.,* p. 71.

37. *Op. cit.,* p. 53.

38. See Winfred Douglas, *Church Music in History and Practice* (rev. ed.; Charles Scribner's Sons, 1962), pp. 163 ff.

39. G. H. Bantock, *Education, Culture and the Emotions* (Faber and Faber, 1967), p. 85.

40. Beacon Press, 1955.

41. *The Church and the Catholic and The Spirit of the Liturgy* (Sheed and Ward, 1935; Ada Lane, tr.), p. 179.

42. *Op. cit.,* p. 19.

43. *Op. cit.,* p. 183.

44. *Op. cit.,* p. 93.

45. Theodore Roszak, "Forbidden Games," in *Technology and Human Values* (Center for the Study of Democratic Values, 1966), p. 28. He is describing the view of Norman O. Brown in *Life Against Death.*

46. (University of Chicago Press, 1963), Ch. 3, "Myth, Cult, and Play."

47. *Philosophy in a New Key* (Mentor Books, 1942), p. 29.

48. *Laws* 653, as quoted by Jane Harrison, *Ancient Art and Ritual* (Henry Holt & Co., 1913), p. 195.

49. Theodore Roszak, *op. cit.*

50. *Op. cit.,* p. 18.

51. *Op. cit.,* p. 104. When von Allmen develops this idea in his article "Worship and the Holy Spirit," *Studia Liturgica* 2 (1963), 124–

135, it is clear he is thinking of ordered games. He is nervous about the possible confusion of sectarian worship in the Spirit, and elaborates "the rules of this play" which "must not be transgressed."

52. *Ibid.,* p. 99.

Chapter 3: Rhythm in the Calendar

1. *Cf.* Walter J. Ong, "Knowledge in Time," *Knowledge and the Future of Man: An International Symposium* (Simon & Schuster Clarion Book, 1968; Walter J. Ong, ed.), pp. 3–38.

2. *Martin Heidegger* ("Makers of Contemporary Theology" Series; D. E. Nineham and E. H. Robertson, eds.; Lutterworth Press, 1968), p. 31.

3. *Confessions* 11, xiv. I have followed the slightly altered translation in Edwyn Bevan, *Symbolism and Belief* (Beacon Press, 1957), p. 84.

4. Pliny, *Epistle* x; Henry Bettenson, ed., *Documents of the Christian Church* (Oxford University Press, 1947), p. 6.

5. See Josef A. Jungmann, *Public Worship* (The Liturgical Press, 1957), p. 231. *Cf.* Jungmann, *The Early Liturgy,* pp. 21 ff; A. Allan McArthur, *The Evolution of the Christian Year* (S.C.M. Press, 1953), Part I.

6. H. B. Porter, *The Day of Light: The Biblical and Liturgical Meaning of Sunday* (The Seabury Press, 1960), pp. 24 ff.

7. "The Book of Sports, 1618" in Bettenson, *Documents,* pp. 389–392. *Cf.* Porter, *op. cit.,* p. 25.

8. Magnesians viii, 9. Cited by Porter, p. 19, *et al.*

9. Apology I, lxvi. Justin's invaluable description of early Christian worship can also be found in Bettenson, *Documents,* pp. 93–95.

10. Following Robert A. Kraft's translation in *Barnabas and the Didache,* Vol. 3 of *The Apostolic Fathers* (Robert M. Grant, ed.; Thomas Nelson & Sons, 1965).

11. Ch. 41; *cf.* Porter, *op. cit.,* p. 20. Willy Rordorf uses this passage to support his argument that Sunday came to be called the Eighth Day *because* baptism was administered then; *Sunday* (Westminster Press, 1968), pp. 275–285.

12. *The Early Liturgy,* p. 23.

13. *Ibid.*

14. Ch. xxvii, 66; *Nicene and Post-Nicene Fathers,* Series 2, Vol. VIII, p. 41. St. Basil also there relates Pentecost to the Eighth Day as a reminder of the Resurrection expected in the Age to Come. *Cf.* McArthur, *op. cit.,* p. 21.

15. Letter 55, *Nicene and Post-Nicene Fathers,* Series 1, Vol. I, p. 304.

16. *De. Civ.* xxii, 30, 5.

17. Barnabas 10:11.

18. *Worship,* p. 225. *Cf.* Paquier, *Dynamics of Worship,* p. 103.

19. I Peter 1:3; *op. cit.,* Ch. V.

20. Abraham Joshua Heschel, *The Sabbath* (Meridian Books, 1963), p. 29.

21. Jungmann, *The Eucharistic Prayer and The Meaning of Sunday* (Fides, 1965), p. 114.

22. *Worship in Israel* (John Knox Press, 1966; Geoffrey Buswell, tr.), pp. 45 ff. Kraus's critique of the overgeneralizing tendencies of phenomenological studies of worship should also be noted, pp. 19 ff.

23. *Cf.* Massey H. Shepherd, Jr., *Liturgy and Education* (The Seabury Press, 1965), p. 98.

24. "The Origins of Christmas," in *The Early Church* (The Westminster Press, 1956).

25. For brief summary of Quartodeciman controversy see S. L. Greenslade, *Schism in the Early Church* (S.C.M. Press, 1953), pp. 99–102. For more recent discussion of the problem as caused by two Jewish calendars, see Jean Daniélou, *The Theology of Jewish Christianity* (Dartman, Longman & Todd, 1964), pp. 343–346; of the controversy as related to the gospels, see Massey H. Shepherd, Jr., *The Paschal Liturgy and The Apocalypse* (John Knox Press, 1960), pp. 41–47.

26. A translation is appended to L. Duchesne, *Christian Worship* (S.P.C.K., 1904), pp. 547–577.

27. McArthur, *op. cit.,* p. 162.

28. *Ibid.,* p. 164.

29. *Ibid.,* p. 165.

30. *Life and Liturgy* (Sheed and Ward Stagbook, 1962), p. 187.

31. *Ibid.,* p. 193.

32. *Ibid.,* p. 196.

33. *An Order of Worship . . . with Commentary* (Consultation on Church Union, 1968), p. 77.

34. *Liturgy and Education,* p. 99. *Cf.* Alexander Schmemann, *Introduction to Liturgical Theology* (American Orthodox Press, 1966), pp. 132 ff. Schmemann is critical of the use of "mystery" language stemming from Dom Odo Casel, and distinguishes this original eschatological theology of time from all later historico-mysterio interpretations.

35. *Ibid.,* p. 100.

36. (Monika B. Vizedom & Gabrielle S. Caffee, trs.; University of Chicago Phoenix Paperback), p. xvii.

37. June 7, 1964.

38. The following summary is based primarily on *The Apostolic Tradition of Hippolytus.* See excerpts of this and other early documents on initiation in Palmer, *Sacraments and Worship,* Part I. *Cf.* Shepherd, *The Paschal Liturgy,* pp. 56 ff.

39. Lecture 2, "On Baptism"; Palmer, p. 19.

40. "A Primitive Christian Baptismal Liturgy," *Essays on New Testament Themes* (S.C.M. Press, 1964; Studies in Biblical Theology No. 41), p. 162.

41. *Ibid.,* p. 168.

Chapter 4: Speaking and Hearing

1. George Steiner, *Language and Silence* (Atheneum, 1967), p. 253. *Cf.* W. Richard Comstock, "Marshall McLuhan's Theory of Sensory Form: A Theological Reflection," *Soundings 51* (1968), pp. 166–181.

2. (University of Toronto Press, 1962), p. 63.

3. *Ibid.,* p. 278.

4. *Ibid.,* p. 267.

5. *Ibid.,* p. 32.

6. *Ibid.,* p. 269.

7. From *The Use of Poetry and the Use of Criticism* (Faber & Faber, 1933), pp. 118–119; as quoted by McLuhan, "Environment as Programmed Happening," in *Knowledge and the Future of Man,* p. 114.

8. *The Gutenberg Galaxy,* p. 45.

9. *A Propos of Lady Chatterley's Lover and Other Essays* (Penguin Books, 1961), pp. 34–35; as quoted by Brian Wicker, *Culture and Liturgy* (Sheed and Ward, 1963), p. 123.

10. Steiner, *op. cit.,* p. 257.

11. *The Sacred Bridge: The Interdependence of Liturgy and Music in Synagogue and Church During the First Millennium* (Columbia University Press, 1959), p. 50.

12. A. Croegaert, *The Mass of the Catechumens* (Cardinal Books, 1963), p. 216.

13. *Ibid.,* p. 214.

14. *Torgau sermon,* 1544, as quoted by William Nicholls, *Jacob's Ladder: The Meaning of Worship* (John Knox Press, 1963; Ecumenical Studies in Worship 4), p. 36.

15. *The Love of Learning and the Desire of God* (Fordham University Press, 1961), pp. 18–19; as quoted by McLuhan, *Gutenberg Galaxy,* p. 89.

16. *Ibid.*

17. Massey Hamilton Shepherd, Jr., *The Reform of Liturgical Worship* (Oxford University Press, 1961), p. 107.

18. Joseph Sittler, *The Ecology of Faith* (Muhlenberg Press, 1961), p. 9.

19. *Ibid.,* p. 8.

20. *Ibid.,* p. 40.

21. *Preaching and Congregation* (John Knox Press, 1962), p. 64.

22. *Worship 38* (1964), 620–625.

23. *Op. cit.,* p. 104.

24. *Ibid.,* p. 3.

25. *Cf.* Herbert Marshall McLuhan, "Address at Vision 65," *The American Scholar 35* (1966), p. 205. See also Remy C. Kwant, *Phenomenology of Language* (Duquesne University Press, 1965).

26. *Op. cit.,* p. 46. *Cf.* Thomas H. Keir, *The Word in Worship* (Oxford University Press, 1962), Ch. 3, "The Image." Keir is one of the few who also recognizes the importance of response from the listeners: "The real ages of great preaching have always been ages of great hearing," p. 5.

27. Millar Patrick, *The Story of the Church's Song* (John Knox Press, 1962; James Sydnor, rev.), p. 72.

28. *Ibid.,* p. 91.

29. Bernard L. Manning, *The Hymns of Wesley and Watts* (The Epworth Press, 1942), p. 12. See also Cecil Northcott, *Hymns in Christian Worship* (John Knox Press, 1965; Ecumenical Studies in Worship 13).

30. *Hymns and the Faith* (Eerdmans Publishing Co., 1968), p. 129.

31. Manning, *op. cit.,* p. 108. *Cf.* Horton Davies, *Worship and Theology in England from Watts and Wesley . . .* (Princeton University Press, 1961), pp. 201–204.

32. *Op. Cit.,* p. 177. A. R. George, "Private Devotion in the Methodist Tradition," *Studia Liturgica 2* (1963), makes the same point when he observes that Methodists rank the hymnbook second only to the Bible as a devotional book, but also that the hymnbook is the document which in practice binds Methodism together, pp. 231–232.

33. *Op. cit.,* p. 33.

34. Robert Guy McCutchan, *Our Hymnody* (The Methodist Book Concern, 1937), p. 12.

35. *Op. cit.,* p. 2.

36. Quoted by Jungmann, *Public Worship,* p. 20.

37. *Phenomenology of Perception,* p. 160.

38. Jungmann, *op. cit.,* pp. 47 and 110; *Cf.* Croegaert, *Mass of the Catechumens,* pp. 126–132.

39. I Apology 67.

40. *Cf.* Jungmann, *op. cit.,* pp. 140 and 133.

41. C. Day Lewis, *The Poetic Image* (Oxford University Press, 1947), p. 99.

Chapter 5: The Sounds of Silence

1. *The Paschal Liturgy and the Apocalypse* (John Knox Press, 1960; Ecumenical Studies in Worship 6), p. 92. Alternatively, he thinks, it might be related to silence in the so-called Prayers of the Faithful in the Eucharist itself.

2. Hom. xvii of *The Liturgical Homilies of Narsai*, as quoted by Charles Harris, "Liturgical Silence," *Liturgy and Worship* (W. K. Lowther Clarke and Harris, eds.; S.P.C.K., 1954), p. 779.

3. Harris, *ibid.*

4. *The Idea of the Holy* (Oxford University Press, 1957), pp. 69, 211.

5. Clarke and Harris, *op. cit.*

6. December 11, 1968.

7. *The Silent Life* (Farrar, Straus & Cudahy, 1957), p. xiii.

8. *Ibid.,* pp. 147–148.

9. *Ibid.,* p. 149.

10. *The Waters of Siloe* (Image Books, 1962), p. 350.

11. *Ibid.,* p. 17.

12. *Ibid.,* p. 350.

13. *Ibid.,* p. 56.

14. *The Silent Life,* p. 36.

15. *Cf.* Appendix VIII, "Silent Worship," *op. cit.,* pp. 210-214.

16. "The Gathered Meeting" (Friends Tract Association, 1946).

17. Canto xxxi, 37–40; Canto xxxiii, 49–108; *The Divine Comedy 3* (Dorothy L. Sayers and Barbara Reynolds, trs.; Penguin Books, 1962). *Cf.* George Steiner, *Language and Silence,* p. 40.

18. John Thomas Nichol, *Pentecostalism* (Harper & Row, 1966), p. 10. Nichol grew up in Pentecostalism, and this background informs his doctoral dissertation detailing the history of the movement.

19. Kilian McDonnell, O.S.B., "The Ecumenical Significance of the Pentecostal Movement," *Worship 40* (1966), 620.

20. Quoted from the Norwegian ed. of Frank Bartleman's memoirs by Nils Bloch-Hoell, *The Pentecostal Movement* (Allen & Unwin, 1964), p. 41.

21. *Ibid.,* p. 42.

22. *Ibid.,* p. 44.

23. *Ibid.,* p. 163.

24. *Ibid.,* p. 161.

25. *Op. cit.,* p. 629.

26. *Ibid.,* p. 615.

27. Bloch-Hoell, *op. cit.,* p. 154.

28. Quoted by Donovan Bess, "The High Church Heresy," *The Nation* (Sept. 28, 1963), p. 174.

29. Quoted by McCandlish Phillips, "And There Appeared to

Them Tongues of Fire," *The Saturday Evening Post* (May 16, 1964), p. 31.

30. Bess, *op. cit.,* p. 175.

31. Phillips, *op. cit.,* p. 32.

32. *Cf.* Finley Eversole, "Man's Extremity and the Modern Artist," *Theology Today 20* (1963–64), 370–389.

33. *Silence* (Wesleyan University Press, 1961), p. 191.

34. *Ibid.,* p. 151.

35. *Ibid.,* p. 154.

36. *Ibid.,* p. 117.

37. *Ibid.,* p. 110.

38. *Op. cit.,* p. 17.

39. *Ibid.,* p. 51.

40. *Ibid.,* p. 52.

41. *Ibid.,* p. 89.

42. *Ibid.,* p. 160.

43. *Ibid.,* p. 168.

44. See Guy Endore, "The Perpetual Stew" (Synanon Foundation, 1968), p. 5.

45. "Address at Vision 65," *The American Scholar 35* (1966), 200.

Chapter 6: Worship and Hope

1. One early example is Walter Lowrie, *Action in the Liturgy* (Philosophical Library, 1953): "we have disparaged hope, which, if it is not the chief tension of the Liturgy, clearly determines the quality of the whole action," p. 45.

2. Martin E. Marty and Dean G. Peerman, eds. (Macmillan, 1968); and *Cross Currents,* Vol. XVIII (1968), 257–335; Walter H. Capps, ed.

3. Charles Davis, *Liturgy and Doctrine* (Sheed and Ward, 1960), Ch. 7.

4. "It Happened Tomorrow," *The New Yorker* (November 16, 1968), p. 237.

5. *The New York Times;* November 12, 1968.

6. Max Born in *Cross Currents* XVI (1966), 257–264. His answer: "Only if we hope do we act in order to bring fulfillment of the hope closer."

7. *Cf.* George Wald's speech with that title, *The New Yorker* (March 22, 1969), pp. 29–31.

8. *Cf.* "The Death of God and the Future of Theology," *The New Christianity* (William Robert Miller, ed.; Delta, 1967), pp. 379–389. Cox also listens to Teilhard de Chardin, whose forward moving thought has, he thinks, similarities to Bloch's.

9. *The Revolution of Hope* (Bantam Books, 1968), p. 54.

10. *Ibid.*, p. 42.

11. *Ibid.*, p. 17.

12. *Ibid.*, p. 19.

13. *Ibid.*, p. 89.

14. *Ibid.*, p. 73.

15. *Ibid.*, p. 145.

16. Hans Frei, *Union Seminary Quarterly Review* XXIII (1968), 267–272.

17. *Theology of Hope* (S.C.M. Press, 1967), p. 194.

18. *Ibid.*, p. 320.

19. *Ibid.*, p. 99.

20. *Ibid.*, p. 161.

21. *Ibid.*, p. 303.

22. Ritschl reports that his manuscript was almost finished when he read Moltmann's *Theologie der Hoffnung,* but he has added some notes in response to this new approach, *op. cit.,* p. vx.

23. *Ibid.*, p. 66.

24. *Ibid.*

25. *Ibid.*, p. 74.

26. *Ibid.*, p. 86.

27. *Ibid.*, p. 169.

28. *Ibid.*, p. 163.

29. "A Theology of Hope: Hope for the Future" (unpublished paper), p. 7.

30. Alexander Schmemann, *Introduction to Liturgical Theology* (The American Orthodox Press, 1966; Asheleigh E. Moorhouse, tr.), p. 59. The rest of the sentence should be noted: "it is also performed within time, and it fills it with new meaning." Schmemann's whole book is an exposition of the eschatology of the Eucharist and its relation to the "liturgy of time." See below, Ch. 7.

Chapter 7: In All Places

1. Robert K. Adair, *Ventures: Magazine of the Yale Graduate School* (Fall, 1968), p. 16.

2. (The Viking Press, 1966), p. 117.

3. *Cf.* Alexander Schmemann, *Introduction to Liturgical Theology,* p. 93.

4. *Ibid.*, p. 135.

5. *Ibid.*, p. 25.

6. B. Bobrinskoy, "Worship and the Ascension of Christ," *Studia Liturgica II* (1963), 108–123. *Cf.* also N. A. Nissiotis, "Worship, Eucharist, and 'Intercommunion': An Orthodox Reflection," *ibid.,* pp. 193–222.

7. Paul Verghese, *The Joy of Freedom: Eastern Worship and Modern Man* (Ecumenical Studies in Worship 17; Lutterworth Press, 1967), p. 38.

8. *Ibid.*, p. 18.

9. *Ibid.*, p. 16.

10. *Physicist and Christian* (The Seabury Press, 1961), p. 98.

11. Richard Paquier, *Dynamics of Worship*, p. 23.

12. Basil Minchin, "The Liturgy and its Setting," in *True Worship*: an Anglo-French Symposium (The Helicon Press, 1963; Lancelot Sheppard, ed.), p. 110.

13. Louis Bouyer, "Jewish and Christian Liturgies"; Sheppard, *op. cit.*, p. 38. In Jerusalem itself, it is worth adding, baptismal candidates renounced Satan while facing west; then turned toward the east while affirming faith in Christ. Cyril of Jerusalem explains this in dark-light symbolism. The same custom was followed in Milan. See Palmer, pp. 16, 27.

14. Minchin, *op. cit.*, p. 110.

15. Josef A. Jungmann, *Public Worship*, p. 17.

16. *Phenomenology of Perception*, p. 251.

17. Colin O. Buchanan, ed. (Oxford University Press, 1968).

18. Quoted by Joyce M. Bennett, "The Diocese of Hong Kong and Macao (The Holy Catholic Church of China)", Buchanan, *op. cit.*, p. 267.

19. John Burgess, "The Church of the Province of Central Africa," *ibid.*, p. 46.

20. Colin F. Bazley, "The Anglican Church of Chile," *ibid.*, pp. 230–239.

21. (Harper & Row, 1963), pp. 1–15.

22. *Cf.* R. Buckminster Fuller, *The American Scholar 35* (1966), 209.

23. *Cf.* Michael Polanyi, *Personal Knowledge* (Harper Torchbook, 1964), pp. 279–286.

Chapter 8: Touch and Feel

1. *Public Worship*, p. 79.

2. *Ibid.*, p. 76. The origin of the tap is uncertain, but it may be a remnant of *The Pax*.

3. "On the Resurrection of the Flesh," 8; Palmer, *op. cit.*, p. 108. In Ch. 9 Tertullian argues for the dignity of the flesh "which God with his own hands constructed in God's image" and to whose rescue he came. *Cf.* Ernest Evans, ed. and tr., *Tertullian's Treatise on the Resurrection* (S.P.C.K., 1960).

4. "Lectures on the Mysteries" III, 3; Palmer, *op. cit.*, p. 22. For an alternative translation see F. L. Cross, ed., *St. Cyril of Jerusalem's Lectures on the Christian Sacraments* (S.P.C.K., 1951), p. 65.

5. "On the Mysteries," VI, 30; Palmer, *op. cit.,* p. 30. The translation in J. H. Srawley, ed., *On the Sacraments and On the Mysteries* (S.P.C.K., 1950), reads *the* priesthood, p. 136.

6. *Ibid.,* VI, 29; Palmer, *op. cit.,* p. 30.

7. *Understanding Media,* p. 67, as quoted by W. Richard Comstock, "Marshall McLuhan's Theory of Sensory Form: A Theological Reflection," *Soundings LI* (1968), 169.

8. *Ibid.,* p. 175.

9. *Ibid.,* p. 178.

10. *Cf.* William C. Schutz, *Joy* (Grove Press, 1968), and George Leonard, *Education and Ecstasy* (Delacorte Press, 1968).

11. William Hamilton, "Two Gurus, or Never Trust Anyone Under 50." *Soundings LI* (1968), 108.

12. *Ibid.,* p. 101. *Cf.* Thomas Altizer's assessment of the earlier work *Life Against Death,* in *Mircea Eliade and the Dialectic of the Sacred,* pp. 169–175.

13. *Love's Body* (Vintage Books, 1966), p. 150.

14. *Ibid.,* p. 121. *Cf.* his 1960 Phi Beta Kappa address at Columbia, "Apocalypse: The Place of Mystery in the Life of the Mind," *Harpers 222* (1961), 46–49.

15. *Ibid.*

16. *Ibid.,* p. 81.

17. *Ibid.,* p. 225.

18. *Ibid.,* p. 127.

19. *Ibid.,* pp. 126, 225.

20. *Ibid.,* p. 221.

21. *Ibid.,* p. 222.

22. *Ibid.,* p. 154.

23. *Ibid.,* p. 214; *cf.* Wheelwright, *The Burning Fountain* (1st ed.), pp. 73–74.

24. *The Human Metaphor* (University of Notre Dame Press, 1964), p. 17.

25. *Ibid.,* p. 41.

26. *Ibid.,* p. 23. *Cf.* Arthur O. Lovejoy's reflections on the ways in which styles of British philosophy reflect changed fashions in English gardens from the 17th to the 19th centuries; "The Study of the History of Ideas," Ch. 1 in *The Great Chain of Being* (Harper Torchbook, 1960).

27. *The Human Metaphor,* p. 63. *Cf.* Michael Polanyi, *Personal Knowledge,* p. 199, where the quotation on the flyleaf of this book is found.

28. *Ibid.,* p. 75. *Cf.* J. Bronowski, "The Logic of the Mind," *The American Scholar 35* (1966), 258–264, where the common quality of imagination in science and the arts is traced to self-reference.

29. *Ibid.,* p. 107.

30. *Ibid.,* p. 84.

31. *Ibid.,* p. 79.

32. *Ibid.*, p. 193.

33. *Ibid.*, p. 198.

34. *Ibid.*, p. 190.

35. From Novalis' fourth "Hymn to Night," as tr. by E. Sewell, *ibid.*, p. 196.

36. Merleau-Ponty, *The Phenomenology of Perception*, pp. 24, 82; *cf.* E. Schillebeeckx, *Christ the Sacrament of Encounter*, p. 64.

37. XVIII, 2, 4; Palmer, *op. cit.*, p. 7.

38. *Apostolic Constitutions* VIII, 11; Palmer, *op. cit.*, p. 78.

39. "On the Mysteries," V, 3; Palmer, *op. cit.*, p. 71.

40. *The Silent Language* (Doubleday & Co., 1959), p. 209.

41. *Cf.* Commentary on *An Order of Worship* (COCU), p. 61.

42. *Cf. Time* (Aug. 2, 1968) report on World Council of Churches.

Chapter 9: Architectural Spaces

1. Jungmann, *The Early Liturgy*, p. 16.

2. Rudolf Schwarz, as quoted by William Alex, "Building for Worship," *The New York Times Book Review* (Dec. 20, 1964), p. 7.

3. E. A. Sovik, "The Role of the Architect in Liturgical Renewal," *Church Architecture: The Shape of Reform* (The Liturgical Conference; Washington, D. C., 1965), p. 20.

4. *Ibid.*, p. 14.

5. Gerald S. Sloyan, "Distribution of Roles and a Renewed Christianity," *op. cit.*, p. 30.

6. André Biéler, *Architecture in Worship* (Oliver & Boyd, 1965), p. 60.

7. Documents on Church Architecture, Appendix to *Church Architecture: The Shape of Reform*, p. 100.

8. Godfrey Diekmann, "The Reformed Liturgy and the Eucharist," *op. cit.*, p. 44.

9. "The Architectural Problem of Protestant Places of Worship," reprinted as an appendix to Biéler, *op. cit.*, p. 93.

10. Diekmann, *op. cit.*, p. 37.

11. Biéler, *op. cit.*, pp. 77–78.

12. *Liturgy and Architecture* (Barrie & Rockliff, 1960), p. 40. *Cf.* also H. Benedict Green, "A Liturgical Brief," in *Towards a Church Architecture* (Peter Hammond, ed.; The Architectural Press, 1962), p. 97.

13. Frédéric Debuyst, *Modern Architecture and Christian Celebration* (Ecumenical Studies in Worship #18; John Knox Press, 1968), p. 57.

14. I Apology 65; Palmer, *op. cit.*, p. 5.

15. Alex, *op. cit.*

16. Quoted from a parish bulletin.

17. *Geography* 9.3.6. I am indebted to my colleague Dr. Georgiana Reynolds for this reference.

18. *The Myth of Eternal Return*, p. 12.

19. Samuel Terrien, "Some Remarks on the Omphalos Myth and Hebrew Religion," Paper presented at the 1968 meeting of the Society of Biblical Literature. *Cf.* Hans-Joachim Kraus, *Worship in Israel*, pp. 201 ff.

20. Alphonse Dupront, "Croisades et eschatologie," as quoted by Eliade, *Myth and Reality*, p. 176.

21. *The Myth of Eternal Return*, p. 20.

22. *Constitution on the Sacred Liturgy*, Ch. I, 8.

23. *Cf.* William L. MacDonald, *Early Christian and Byzantine Architecture* (George Braziller, 1962), p. 36.

24. James Dougherty, "The Church and the Image of the City," *Cross Currents 16* (1966), 395–415.

25. *Cf.* William F. Lynch, *Images of Hope* (Mentor-Omega, 1965); see also Karl Rahner, "Christianity and the New Earth," in *Knowledge and the Future of Man*, pp. 255–268; and "Christian Humanism," *Journal of Ecumenical Studies IV* (1967), 369–384.

26. Frank Kacmarcik, *Church Architecture: The Shape of Reform*, p. 77. *Cf.* Joost de Blank, "A church which is inward-looking is really no church at all," quoted by R. Aled Davies, "Liturgy and the Mission of the Church," in *The Renewal of Worship* (Ronald C. D. Jasper, ed.; Oxford University Press, 1965), p. 76.

27. *The World and the Person* (Henry Regnery, 1965), p. 75.

28. (Delachaux et Niestlé, 1963), p. 126.

29. *Ibid.*, p. 141.

30. *Introduction to Liturgical Theology*, p. 94.

31. Karl Rahner, *Theological Investigations IV*, p. 331, as quoted by Hans Küng, *The Church* (Sheed and Ward, 1968), p. 67.

32. Küng, *op. cit.*, p. 88.

33. *Ibid.*, p. 92.

Chapter 10: Taste and See

1. The Epitaph of Abercius, Bishop of Hierapolis, ca. 200; Palmer, *op. cit.*, p. 199.

2. Gregory Dix, tr.; Bard Thompson, *Liturgies of the Western Church*, p. 21.

3. "On the Crown," 3; Palmer, *op. cit.*, p. 275.

4. "On the Mysteries," 4.9; 5.21; Palmer, *op. cit.*, pp. 25, 75.

5. Apology I, 66; *ibid.*, p. 5.

6. Letter 63.

7. "On the Mysteries" viii. 43. 58; Palmer, *op. cit.*, pp. 32, 36.

8. Didache 10; *ibid.*, p. 3.

9. *Let Us Now Praise Famous Men* (Houghton Mifflin, 1960), p. 89.

10. *Ibid.,* p. 90.

11. (Dacre Press, 1945), p. xiv.

12. Basil Minchin, "The Liturgy and its Setting," *True Worship* (Lancelot Sheppard, ed.; The Helicon Press, 1963), p. 108.

13. Dix, *op. cit.,* p. 228. *Cf.* George Every, *Basic Liturgy: A Study in the Structure of the Eucharistic Prayer* (The Faith Press, 1961).

14. *The Lutheran Liturgy* (Muhlenberg Press, 1947), p. 218.

15. *Short Treatise,* as quoted by C. W. Dugmore, "The Eucharist in the Reformation Era," *Eucharistic Theology Then and Now* (S.P.C.K., 1968), p. 71. *Cf.* Peter Brooks, *Thomas Cranmer's Doctrine of the Eucharist* (The Seabury Press, 1965), p. 71.

16. Brooks, *op. cit.,* p. 103.

17. *Cf.* "Resume of the Emerging Consensus on the Eucharist", issued by "Information Documentation on the Conciliar Church" (St. Louis Review, 1969). It includes texts drawn from World Council of Churches Faith and Order Commission meetings from 1952–1967.

18. On this subject see C. B. Naylor, "Eucharistic Theology Today," *Eucharistic Theology Then and Now,* pp. 106–116; Pope Paul VI's encyclical, Mysterium Fidei (September, 1965); and *Intercommunion Today* (Church of England Information Office, 1968), esp. p. 65. *Cf.* E. C. Ratcliff, "The English Use of Eucharistic Consecration: 1548–1662," *Theology 60* (1957), 229–236; 273–280.

19. *Cf.* Joachim Jeremias, *The Eucharistic Words of Jesus* (Blackwell, 1955), pp. 73 ff.

20. J. D. Crichton, "An Historical Sketch of the Roman Liturgy," in Sheppard, *True Worship,* pp. 63–64.

21. *Cf.* Cyril of Jerusalem, "On the Mysteries," 5.20; Palmer, p. 75.

22. *Modern Architecture and Christian Celebration,* pp. 10–11.

23. *The Eastern Orthodox Church* (Aldine Publishing Co., 1963), p. 24; italics mine.

24. Jeremias, *op. cit.,* p. 174.

25. Paul Verghese, *The Joy of Freedom,* p. 63.

26. *Ibid.,* p. 64.

27. *Ibid.,* p. 58.

28. Philip Sherrard, "The Art of the Icon," *Sacrament and Image* (A. M. Allchin, ed.; The Fellowship of St. Alban & St. Sergius, 1967), p. 58.

29. *The Meaning of Icons* (Boston Book and Art Shop, 1952), p. 29.

30. Benz, *op. cit.,* p. 6.

31. *Ibid.,* p. 8.

32. As quoted in Heinz Skrobuche, *Icons* (Dufour Editions, 1965), p. 10.

33. Third Discourse in Defense of the Holy Icons, 16; cited in Skrobuche, *op. cit.,* p. 10.

34. *Cf.* Ouspensky, *op. cit.,* p. 37.

35. *Op. cit.,* p. 52.

36. "Explanation of the Divine Liturgy," pamphlet originally issued by the Greek Orthodox Church in Minneapolis, Minn. Italics mine.

37. "The Catholic Dream World and the Sacred Image," *Worship 35* (1960–61), 559.

38. *Ibid.,* p. 554.

39. *Early Christian Worship* (Studies in Biblical Theology #10; Alec R. Allenson, 1953).

Chapter 11: The Breaking of Images

1. *Truth and Symbol* (Twayne Publishers, 1959; Jean T. Wilde, William Kluback and Walter Kimmel, trs.), p.60.

2. Edward James Martin, *A History of the Iconoclastic Controversy* (S.P.C.K., 1933), p. 22.

3. G. E. von Grunebaum, "Byzantine Iconoclasm and the Influence of the Islamic Environment," *History of Religions 2* (1962), p. 5. *Cf.* Martin, *op. cit.,* p. 134.

4. Martin, *op. cit.,* pp. 50–51.

5. *Ibid.,* p. 129.

6. *The Dynamics of Faith* (Harper & Row, 1957), p. 104.

7. *Cf., e.g.,* Eugeny Lampert, *The Divine Realm* (Faber & Faber, 1944).

8. Martin, *op. cit.,* pp. 103–104.

9. *Commentaries on the Four Last Books of Moses* (Wm. B. Eerdmans, 1950), Vol. II, p. 195.

10. *The Waning of the Middle Ages* (Edward Arnold & Co., 1924), p. 182.

11. *Ibid.,* p. 140.

12. *Ibid.,* p. 182. He is quoting Gerson.

13. Calvin, *op. cit.,* p. 390.

14. *Ibid.,* p. 173.

15. *Ibid.,* p. 116.

16. *Ibid.,* p. 121.

17. *Ibid.,* p. 109.

18. *Ibid.,* p. 124.

19. C. B. Moss, *The Church of England and the Seventh Council* (The Faith Press, 1957), p. 34.

20. (Hodder and Stoughton, n.d.; ca. 1913), pp. 280–281.

21. Jean-Philippe Ramseyer, *La Parole et l'image,* p. 46.

22. *Ibid.,* p. 78.

23. *Constitution on the Sacred Liturgy,* Ch. VII.

24. J. D. Crichton, *The Church's Worship,* p. 234.

25. Cloud H. Meinberg, "The Baptistry and Other Spaces," *Worship 35* (1960–61), pp. 536–549.

26. Canon 18 of the Council of Gangra, ca. 358, as quoted in A. Allan McArthur, *The Evolution of the Christian Year*, p. 21.

27. "On Fasting," as cited *ibid.*, p. 24.

28. *Ibid.*, p. 23.

29. *The Pilgrimage of Etheria*, IV. 5.

30. *Cf.* Shepherd of Hermas, *Sim.*, v.1.1–2.

31. *The Brothers Karamazov* (Modern Library Edition), p. 301; quoted by Gabriel Vahanian, *Wait Without Idols* (George Braziller, 1964), p. 191.

32. "To Keep a True Lent," *The Poetical Works of Robert Herrick* (L. C. Martin, ed.; Clarendon Press, 1956), p. 391.

33. *The Daily Californian* (Nov. 11, 1968).

34. Vahanian, *op. cit.*, p. 50.

35. *Ibid.*, p. 30. *Cf.* his "Christianity's Lost Iconoclasm," *The Nation 192* (1961), 354–357.

36. *Ibid.*, p. 230.

37. *Ibid.*, p. 184.

38. "For the Time Being," *Collected Poetry* (Random House, 1945), p. 413.

39. W. Richard Comstock, "Theology After the 'Death of God,'" *Cross Currents XVI* (1966), 294.

40. Simone Weil, *Gravity and Grace*, p. 104; as quoted by Comstock, *ibid.*

41. Schoenberg's "Moses and Aaron"; George Steiner, *Language and Silence*, p. 135.

42. *Cf.* Norman O. Brown, *Love's Body*, p. 222.

43. *Ibid.*, p. 247.

Chapter 12: Worship and Action

1. See, *e.g.*, Howard G. Hageman, "Liturgy and Mission," *Theology Today XIX* (1962), 169–170.

2. (Oxford University Press, 1967), p. 178.

3. *Ibid.*, p. 96.

4. *Culture and Liturgy* (Sheed and Ward, 1963), p. 44.

5. Robert E. Cushman, "Worship as Acknowledgment," in Shepherd, ed., *Worship in Scripture and Tradition*, pp. 9–43.

6. E. Schillebeeckx, *Christ the Sacrament of Encounter with God* (Sheed and Ward, 1963), p. 214.

7. Gabriel Vahanian, *Wait Without Idols*, p. 109.

8. *Cf.* Louis MacNeice, "Autumn Journal," as quoted by C. Day Lewis, *The Poetic Image*, p. 110.

9. James A. Pike, "Why I'm Leaving the Church," *Look 33* (Apr. 29, 1969), p. 55.

10. *Anatomy of Criticism* (Princeton University Press, 1957), p. 76.

11. *Ibid.*, p. 111.

12. *Cf.* Hans Küng, *The Church,* pp. 59, 69.

13. Mt. 27:51 ff.

14. Charles Henderson, "An Electric Circus of the Spirit," *World Outlook XXIX* (1969), 14–17.

15. I. Thess. 5:19.

16. Anthony Schillaci, "Film as Environment," *Saturday Review* (Dec. 28, 1968), pp. 8 ff.

17. Jaspers, *Truth and Symbol,* p. 60.

INDEX

199

RELATED TITLES BY SEABURY:

LITURGY FOR LIVING by Charles P. Price and Louis Weil. Church Teaching Series Volume Five. "Firmly rooted in scripture and in teaching of the Church Fathers. Not only does the Bible emerge as a liturgical resource of the utmost importance, but its vitality is seen to carry on in the living liturgical life of the church."—*Canadian Churchmen*

S-0422-4		368 pp.
S-2218-4	paperback	368 pp.
S-2225-7	Use Guide	40 pp.

SANCTIFYING LIFE, TIME, AND SPACE: An Introduction to Liturgical Study by Marion J. Hatchett. "A complete and concise guide to the Christian liturgical tradition."—*Christian Bookseller*

"For seminarians, lay study groups."—*Choice*

S-0290-6   224 pp.

COMMENTARY ON THE AMERICAN PRAYER BOOK by Marion J. Hatchett. "This companion to the *1979 Book of Common Prayer* 'explains' the new Prayer Book, the history of each section, all the whys and wherefores—page by page."—*The Episcopalian*

S-0206-X   688 pp.

INTRODUCING THE LESSONS OF THE CHURCH YEAR: A Guide for Lay Readers and Congregations by Frederick Houk Borsch. Includes the three year cycle of lessons, a text variation guide, lesson introductions and public reading hints. "Rare is the lay reader so well-versed in the Bible, so at ease at the lectern, who . . . will not benefit from this."—*Library Journal*

S-0396-1   240 pp.

PATTERNS OF PRAYER IN THE PSALMS by Laurence Dunlop. A book of great value for those who regularly use the Psalms in prayer. Throughout, the Psalms are seen as examples of prayer into which twentieth century Christians can enter. Exegetical questions are not ignored, and there are helpful explanations of Basic Hebrew terms and concepts. Laurence Dunlop is a priest and is Assistant Professor of Theology at Loyola University of Chicago.

S-2377-6   192 pp.